PRACTIC OF SEX

The subject of sex, sex positions and sex methods

Jack Bracknell

Contents

Annotation

Is sex really something to learn? Definitely yes! Is it hard to imagine that sex in a long-term marriage can still be fraught with pleasant surprises? Think variety in bed means changing partners? And why not start to comprehend the art of love ... from yourself? Sex is not only a technique. This is the ability to confess love– virtuoso and with feeling!

- What if sex does not bring joy? – 7 types of female orgasm – how to achieve them? - How to diversify marital sex? - Is the third not superfluous? And the fourth? – Pros and cons of sex experiments – Sex for love or love for sex? - Friendship and sex - how to combine?

Introduction

It would seem that tons of manuals have already been written on sex. They perfectly explain what, where, how, in what position and in what interior. And why and when, it is left to everyone to decide according to their own understanding. At the same time, in fact, it turns out that one of the most important and interesting areas of our life raises many questions that, it seems, there is no one to ask. It's not for mom and dad to be interested, in fact? Even if you get over your embarrassment, the answer may be like talking to a medieval barber about epilators. And all because everyone has stereotypes and myths of different eras intertwined in their heads. Even in our relatively free time, you can get completely confused and add a complete set of strangers to your complexes.

From what point of view will we talk about sex in this book? We will touch on the technical side of the matter in passing and minimally, because everything has already been written many times before us, and this is not the task of the book. The main thing is to understand what ideas about sex exist, which of them prevent us from living a full and happy life, which, perhaps, are even useful.

The subject of sex is a delicate one, although it is thankfully not as embarrassing as it was just a few decades ago. All information is in the public domain, and books and the Internet, as well as the stories of girlfriends, expand the boundaries of our perception and horizons in the most unexpected directions.

So, we will not impose high moral principles on you and evaluate this or that concept related to the intimate sphere of life from the standpoint of morality or religious attitudes. We, as the classic used to say, "Let's go a different way" and ask only two questions: the first - "Does it harm you?" The second - "Does it harm others?" And the answers to these questions may well give you a clear understanding of the admissibility or inadmissibility (for you personally, of course) of this or that type of sex and everything connected with it.

In general, there will be no arguments like "All progressive people do THIS" here, as well as statements like "Only perverts do THIS", because in all of us there is a little from both of them, and then we all adults and no one is obliged to report on their preferences.

But let's talk in detail about how sex affects family life. The topic is up to date! A record number of letters to the editors of "Cleo" comes with requests for help:

"Why is he cheating?", "Why is he not paying attention to me?" and "We are fine, except for the bed, what should we do?"

Let's talk about those sex-related things that annoy us, about taking sex too seriously and contraception too frivolously, about how important it is to pay attention to this area of life and not put off solving problems “until later”, and how, in the end Finally, to get more pleasure from this process. About what diversity in sex gives us, what reasons make spouses cheat on each other, and what interesting things have been invented over many centuries in this area, read in the book?

Chapter 1

In Soviet times, they also paid attention to the educational program in the field of intimate relationships and published brochures where sexologists told what problems patients came to them with and how to improve the sex life of newlyweds. Most of all, I was shocked by the real story, when the couple, after two years of marriage, asked for help, because the woman could not get pregnant. And through questioning, it turned out that they, as one anecdote says, "Took all this time for an orgasm asthma attacks," that is, practically penetration did not occur, but for some reason they did not bother to find out how to do it.

Such stories clearly make it clear that instincts do not always work and you should not rely on them alone, but you should, as they say on the Internet, "study the materiel" - and first in theory. Before driving a car, we are trained, before the birth of a child, we learn how to care for him so as not to harm. But with sex somehow it is not accepted. There doesn't seem to be anything to learn...In fact, this "simple act" has so many nuances that you can explore it all your life. Moreover, everything happens differently for different people, and even with age, habits, desires, reactions of the body are constantly changing.

The theory is also different. Many hopefully grab

onto the Kama Sutra, and there are only poses and tips that are more interesting from a literary point of view. Learning from porn movies, as teenagers do, is also not the best option. Firstly, they mount most of these pictures from cutting a mass of takes to make it more spectacular, but we want to have sex for pleasure, and not for some invisible observer. Secondly, having sex for several hours in a row, as well as constantly changing partners, is very difficult. Porn actors, turning sex into their work, for a long time lose the ability to enjoy it. And then, you never know, like everyone else, what if it's me who doesn't succeed at all?

My boyfriend doesn't satisfy me

My boyfriend and I have been together for four years, of which we have been living together for three years. We love each other and, probably, we no longer imagine ourselves apart. I satisfy him regularly and in any form in which he wants. It's different with me. Four years ago, when we started dating, neither of us had had a sexual experience. At first, I began to succeed in satisfying my boyfriend. I didn't feel anything special. Then it started to strain us and I already began to think that I was frigid, the guy began to blame his short penis. No poses for such cases, which are usually written about, did not help. Then everything began to improve and I began to feel that we had chosen a good position. But as soon as I start to feel during the act, I start to breathe hard or moan, he immediately ends! We agreed that this would not work, first I will satisfy him, and then we will proceed to the act itself, so that it lasts longer. And just yesterday, during the desired action, he tells me: “You gave me such an awesome blowjob that now I don’t feel anything.” Every time we have something new. He says that he really wants to satisfy me and feels like an inferior man, but in the end there are no changes. There are no problems other than this one. And I want sex. I’m only 21 years old, and sometimes I’ll be so tight that I don’t know what to do with myself. Advise, please, something, very much I ask.

That really wants to satisfy me and feels like an inferior man, but in the end, no changes. There are no problems other than this one. And I want sex. I'm only 21 years old, and sometimes I'll be so tight that I don't know what to do with myself. Advise, please, something, very much I ask that really wants to satisfy me and feels like an inferior man, but in the end, no changes. There are no problems other than this one. And I want sex. I'm only 21 years old, and sometimes I'll be so tight that I don't know what to do with myself. Advise, please, something, very much I ask.

Marina, Moscow, 21 years old

Alyona:

Marina, as I understand it, only you have been involved in sexual education for all four years, and your boyfriend, despite his words about love and the desire to satisfy you, has not done anything in this direction during this time and is simply sure that the only tool to satisfy a woman that a man possesses is an erect penis. Alas, your boyfriend is either not that smart or lazy. You have quite openly discussed the technique of sex in a couple, you agree and experiment, but you take an active position in these matters. He really is deeply violet, what you feel there and what you want. If it were otherwise, then you wouldn't be jumping around him, making him "good" by all means at hand, but he would be trying to satisfy you, using the same hands, lips and tongue, since he himself believes that his male organ is not so big. But the problem is that for some reason he does not want to do this. Favorably accepting caresses from you, he does not consider it necessary to answer you in the same way. If I were you, I would ask the question: "Why?"

After all, a woman can get a full-fledged orgasm in the same way as a man, without direct sexual intercourse. Has your boyfriend thought of this? Then it's time. Whatever your relationship in all other planes, but if you continue to please him without getting sexual release yourself, you will still run away from him. Although, maybe it's for the best. For I do not believe that a guy loves you so much, since for so many years he himself has not bothered to give you pleasure in sex. You suit him, of course, because you are relaxed, well-read and do "awesome blowjobs." But in this area of relationships, you don't have reciprocity. And this will be the worm that will eat your "apple" from the inside.

Sergey:

Marina, the only thing I can advise you is to change your partner. A man who, in three years of marriage, has not figured out how to please his woman, simply does not want it. And if he doesn't want to, then he doesn't really love him very much. After all, anyone can simply move the lower back in a certain rhythm. But if a guy really wanted to please you, he found out long ago that only 30% of women can enjoy frictions. All the rest, in order to achieve relaxation, need to stimulate the clitoris, which does not need a member at all. But gentle fingers and tongue - very even. That is why the size of the penis, in general, is completely unimportant.

The main thing is that the head is in place and the hands. If he really doesn't want to give you pleasure with his mouth or fingers, then this is how he really treats you. And instead of giving blowjobs to such a gentleman, getting into exotic poses and blaming yourself for frigidity, you just need to find a person who will first of all take care of your pleasure, and only then of his own. It's only in the movies that the main characters have sex in a missionary position and always get a mutual one-time orgasm. In life, this happens very rarely. More often, after all, one of the partners "finishes" first, and then gives pleasure to the second. Your boyfriend has the audacity to say that after a blowjob he does not feel anything that is, go to hell with your desires, I want to sleep! So you think all the same, do you need such a passenger? If you still need it for some reason, then try to explain to him that he can work with other parts of the body in the same way to make you feel good. Buy pornographic films, after all, and see how it's done. Only something tells me that the guy still does not want to strain. And if so, then drop it as soon as possible. Nothing good will come of it with such a partner.

I don't satisfy him.

I am dating a young man who is eight years older than me, but this does not bother us, we have excellent relations: I have with his family, he has established contact with mine. Everything was fine: he fulfilled all my desires, dates, romance - in general, everything. I also tried to "look after" him: I cooked breakfast (sometimes we spend the night together), did laundry, helped around the house, we didn't even really quarrel with him (there were misunderstandings, no more than a day, even in two hours we resolved all conflicts). But today I learned something: in an intimate sense, I do not satisfy him, he is my first, but he found out only after everything had already happened (I was embarrassed). Sometimes it hurts me, but I endure. More recently, he began to understand this. Yesterday we had, I was hurt, I was silent, he understood and pretended that he had finished, and today he told me that he had deceived me. How can I be now, how to satisfy him? Sex is one of the most important criteria in a relationship...

Marusya, Volgograd, 18 years old

Alyona:

Marusya, there are many ways to solve your problem. Only it is necessary to solve it, and not sit and worry about it. And decide together. Your young man should also think: if you experience pain during sex and are patiently silent, then what kind of sex is it between two loving people? He's just using you for physical release. Maybe your man is also tense about this? The fact that he is eight years older than you does not automatically make him more experienced and skilled. Rather, the opposite is true - judging by your feelings during sex, your beloved is not a great master in bed, otherwise he would know how to receive and give pleasure without causing pain. And I advise you not to look for advice on forums, but to do the elimination of sexual illiteracy. Now you can find a lot of books about the technique of sex, and very sensible and not at all vulgar. Learn and adopt what you find acceptable. But, I repeat, it would be good for your man to read them too, because a man who tells a woman that she does not satisfy him in sex, most likely, is nothing of himself in bed.

A man who tells a woman that she does not satisfy him in sex, most likely, is nothing of himself in bed.He is probably one of those males who are sure that a woman should get incredible pleasure from the sexual intercourse itself, and does not bother to look for other options.

Sergey:

Marusya, from the point of view of physiology, there is not a single woman in this world who could not satisfy a man sexually. This is just unreal. This is because a man gets pleasure from stimulating a very specific part of the body. And the method of stimulation is not particularly important. Another thing is that experience, knowledge and a certain originality in the process of stimulation by a woman give the process some sophistication and additional impressions. The ability to caress with hands, mouth, buttocks, breasts, and other delights - all this enhances the impressions received by a man. That is why, by the way, Greek getters, Japanese geishas, as well as other representatives of the oldest profession, who did not even differ in outstanding forms, have always been appreciated by any representatives of the male population. Moreover, many of them were made queens.

This I mean that you simply cannot not satisfy your friend. However, one should also not forget that the above ladies received a very substantial payment for their work and knowledge. That is why they were ready to give themselves. It was a job that paid well. After all, the woman herself did not understand what she received. And everyone understood this very well. But also do not forget that not a single real geisha or hetaera could become one without gaining experience with a real man. Because only he can awaken in a woman the desire to have sex. Only he, with his concern for the satisfaction of, first of all, his partner, knowledge, or at least the desire for this, could awaken sensuality and show what is good in sex. And you in this regard, alas, have not been lucky yet. Your friend is a commonplace consumer. He simply does "frictions", waiting for your violent reaction, not even assuming that 70% of women from this action do not get anything but irritation of the mucous membrane. Yes, and takes offense at this, accusing you of frigidity.

So, Marusya, let me open your eyes to the sex life, which is really one of the cornerstones of relationships. A real, loving man thinks first of all about the satisfaction of his partner, and only then about his own.

A real, loving man thinks first of all about the satisfaction of his partner, and only then about his own.

In order for sex not to bring pain, for this he must use his head and hands first. And if a man believes that 16-20 centimeters of cavernous bodies filled with blood and half an hour of continuous contractions of the lumbar muscles is enough for all the ladies to immediately faint, then send such a gentleman to hell. He only thinks of himself. And if so, then you risk wasting time without getting real pleasure from sex. Moreover, your friend is already 26 years old and he simply cannot help but know what and how is happening in this regard. And since he did not bother to find out your sensitive areas, or at least ask if you had a sexual relationship before, it means that this is how he treats you. No, it's definitely up to you to decide. I understand that this is your first man and you think that he is ideal. But actually it is not.

In reality, not everyone manages to adapt to each other immediately, especially if both partners are inexperienced people and not savvy in theory. True, some can form a family at the age of 18 and solve all issues together, while others scatter in search of someone more "Technical", but the truth lies in the fact that some love each other and want to learn how to give each other pleasure, while others are interested in trying to get an orgasm, but not bothering about giving pleasure to a partner.

Numerous prejudices also come into play here.

Consider the example of several myths, their impact on relationships.

MYTH 1: All people are the same in their sexual habits.

Every teenager rediscovers this truth, as do many others. A man is used to pleasing one woman with a certain set of actions: first kissing, then biting on the ear, for example, and then - according to the usual scenario. And then she meets another woman and repeats her gentlemanly set, and her ear is not an erogenous zone, she actually doesn't like it. In a good way, all this can be quickly felt and rebuilt, to hear the hints of a woman, in the end. But there are men who do not want to rebuild (maybe the main thing for him is to change partners more often, and not to study their desires - waste time) or even does not come to mind! Judging by the books and films, again, it can be assumed that all types of caresses evoke a uniquely positive reaction - and everyone has the same. But no! One needs to be spanked the other only needs gentle strokes, the third wants to be bitten and scratched, and another part of the women do not understand what they want at all. The same applies to men. They themselves may not know about half of their erogenous zones, because they have not met a woman who would show initiative and imagination.

That is why sex with a new, yet unknown partner is so attractive for most people. Imagine: another person will act unconventionally towards you, maybe give unusual impressions and sensations, reveal new potential in you ... For the sake of a variety of impressions, people commit adultery if there is nothing surprising with a husband or wife for a long time. True, there is no guarantee that the other man will be better, but a change of impressions will definitely be provided.

It is precisely because of the difference in the perception of the same factors and actions that it is not easy to find harmony in sex. You need to learn on your own, perhaps teach your partner, try something unusual for you and show your imagination ... And these initiatives should come from both sides. You need to learn on your own, perhaps teach your partner, try something unusual for you and show your imagination and these initiatives should come from both sides.

Not only that, as soon as you get used to each other and study each other's reactions, it would seem, comprehensively and forever, as it turns out that you have changed. And you have to adapt to new circumstances. What are the changes? For example, you went to work and began to communicate with new people, felt more confident and began to manage your subordinates, and involuntarily brought these habits of command into your personal life. And in sex, too, began to behave a little more aggressively. Or you are in a romantic mood, hormones act in such a way that you want to cry and only tenderness. And the old-fashioned husband insists on violent quick sex.

And how childbirth affects a woman - it’s hard for

a man to imagine! Everything changes: hormonal levels, physiology, everyday circumstances, and emotions. A woman tries on a new role - a mother, but this role is not associated with sex, the images of wife and mother need to be reconciled with each other, learn how to combine. If the head is full of caring for the child, and the maternal instincts are at full capacity in the first months after childbirth, it is difficult to reconfigure the husband. Much depends on the woman, has its own nuances, which depend on how the birth went, how quickly the body recovers, whether the baby is healthy, whether the mother helps with the housework, etc.

Childbirth, again, can leave a serious psychological trauma, as a result of which sexual intercourse causes unpleasant associations with the experience and the fear of becoming pregnant again, and not at all joy and pleasure, as it was before. If a woman gave birth lying on her back, for example, it is better for her not to use such a position in sex so that nothing reminds of the delivery room.

In the first month after childbirth, sex is generally under a medical ban, but in the next six months it can be extremely painful if the birth was traumatic. No, don't be scared, this doesn't apply to all women, but it happens. And then it is more and more difficult to return to the previous intimate relationship with her husband. The appearance of a woman most often changes, "internal" - too. The muscles of the vagina are stretched, and the sensations of both participants in the process are already different. It happens that it is required to carry out intimate plastic surgery to return the old sensations. There are other ways, which will be discussed in later chapters.

Where did sex go after childbirth?

I have such a problem: I gave birth to a child six months ago, I have known my husband for less than three years, we have been married for two years, our relationship has always been tender and trusting, and my husband really wanted a child, so we prepared, planned and were very happy about my pregnancy. But the pregnancy was problematic, the doctors recommended to exclude sex, which we did. And now six months have passed since the birth of my daughter, many difficulties have been experienced, relations with her husband are good, but there is still no sex. There were several attempts, so to speak, but then the child woke up, then the sight of milk pouring from the chest discouraged her husband, then what a trifle, in the end, nothing worked out. We lie down in bed, hug tightly - and sleep. I am already in despair, it seems to me that my husband simply does not want me, and I don't know what I should do. I have a complex, wind myself up, I have lost a lot of weight, become angular, plus milk.

But I always thought that men do not pay attention to such trifles, and then there is such a huge period without sex. Having another woman can't imagine because he To help me straight home from work, I know all his income and expenses, well, that is, I can't imagine how it is possible, if he doesn't have free time and expenses, to get someone. He assures me that everything is fine, that the baby will grow up and everything will get better, but I don't understand: where is it normal, it doesn't happen, I want him to show interest in me. And if there is still another woman, then what should I do? And in general, does it happen that a man does not crave sex?

Lena, Ukraine, 33 years old

Alyona:

It is a delusion to consider all men without exception as preoccupied rabbits who do not care about the atmosphere and "little things" in sex. Childbirth changes not only a woman, but also her man. Especially if he was admitted to the very process of the birth of a child and saw the whole physiological side of the birth of a baby. Even if not, some men may indeed not have sexual desire for their wife for some time after the birth of a child. But not because she became disgusting to him, but because her role as a mother temporarily overshadowed all her other roles in the family. Well, indeed, milk leaking from the breast may not be the best incentive in such a situation.

In my opinion, if you are confident in your husband, if he shows care, attention, if you sleep in an embrace, then you just need to give time to your couple. The child is growing, you will not breastfeed him indefinitely. Undermine him at night - too. So, you will gradually enter a more familiar rut for your couple. As far as I understand, you have already discussed this issue with your husband, and he actually told you the same thing. Just one piece of advice: you don't need to passively wait for a certain moment when passion "turns on" again. Try to show your husband signs of attention (and unobtrusively ask him for the same): simple gestures, contacts, looks that confirm your physical closeness to each other - stroke your cheek, hug, put your hand on your shoulder, gently run your hand through your hair, etc. e. All this can be done legally in the presence of a child, and it all fuels the physical contact between you and your husband. In addition, in order to have sex with such a small child, it is not at all necessary to wait for the night, nor is it necessary to be completely naked (so as not to demonstrate lactating breasts). The child sleeps during the day too, the husband has days off, and a scantily clad woman looks much sexier than completely naked. That is, I personally advocate not to wind yourself up, not to panic, but to quietly experiment and restore physical and erotic contact with your husband. And a half-dressed woman looks much sexier than a completely naked one. That is, I personally advocate not to wind yourself up, not to panic, but to quietly experiment and restore physical and erotic contact with your husband. And a half-dressed woman looks much sexier than a completely naked one. That is, I personally advocate not to wind yourself up, not to panic, but to quietly experiment and restore physical and erotic contact with your husband.

Sergey:

Lena, we are all people, we are all different, and therefore everything happens in life. And the reluctance to have sex with a pregnant or nursing wife is also a relative norm. Not for everyone, of course, but still there are quite a few such men. So I don't think you should be too nervous about this. However, why don't you change your sexual behavior a bit if the situation bothers you? In conditions when a certain order of things has developed, it is possible to wait for its change in the hope that everything will work itself out for a very long time. So just start behaving outside the box. For example, try to "rape" your husband without any preparation and other conventions. And at an unusual time and not in a marital bed. So say: they say, everything, dear, I want you right here and now and without any objections. Then dump it on any horizontal surface and sit on top. And if he is embarrassed by the sight of milk flowing from the breast or the sagging breast itself, then it is not at all necessary to completely undress. A beautiful translucent bust - and everything is fine. In addition, do not forget that you can give a man pleasure not only in the standard way. This can also be done with the hands or mouth. And yes, you also need to enjoy yourself. So ask your husband to please you. And also how he can. It won't work with a penis - he has hands and a tongue. And in the process of this action, the "unbearable" And yes, you also need to enjoy yourself. So ask your husband to please you. And also how he can. It won't work with a penis - he has hands and a tongue. And in the process of this action, the "unbearable" And yes, you also need to enjoy yourself. So ask your husband to please you. And also how he can. It won't work with a penis - he has hands and a tongue. And in the process of this action, the "unbearable "can jump up like a little one. The main thing here is to break the stereotype. Yes, and an active desire on the part of the wife sometimes works better than any aphrodisiac. Well, then things can really get better on their own. So do not grieve and do not lose weight unnecessarily. Some men also want to hold on to something soft, and not just prick on their knees.

The fact that even one person in his life can change tastes and habits, and even more so that they differ in all people, must be accepted and used to your advantage. Do you think what is the secret of married couples who have not bothered each other for decades? In change. Both spouses are constantly changing, as soon as something gets boring, they invent something new, change their appearance and the standard set of caresses for something else. If your husband occupies a significant place in your life and you like everything about him, but sex has become annoying, change yourself, and your husband will catch up. If, of course, he loves. And if you still love him.

Of course, it's easy to say... And if you really, really can't bear the intimacy with your husband, who used to be so dear? Figure it out, ask yourself honestly and frankly: what went wrong and when?

First, when did it all start? Were there quarrels, scandals, maybe the husband behaved somehow especially ugly? Or changed? Or just disappointed? If not, are you simply bored? Has your marriage entered a stage where the violent passion fades and everything becomes mundane? So keep in mind that this is a natural process and, by the way, reversible. But if there is no more love, then there is nothing to save. But many women write that they love their husband very much, the children adore their dad, the house is a full bowl and life is a success, but with sex it's stressful. And even attempts to dress up in red underwear do not give the desired effect. And I want everything to be perfect with my own husband, and not with a stray lover.

I don't want to have sex with him anymore

We live with a common-law husband for almost two years. Recently, I started having problems with passion. At first, the prelude was shortened, then it completely disappeared, and then on my part it was like a marriage debt, nothing more. Now I don't want sex at all. With my husband, I like to spend time, wallow, lisp, and when it comes to the very thing, it becomes a burden for me. All this lasted about a month, then he generally stopped hinting at anything like that, apparently tired. Another week has passed, and now I understand that I can do without his kisses and caresses. Moreover - I do not want this sex at all. And we live like neighbors... Who is on TV, who is on PC. On the other hand, I think: well, why don't you come up, don't try, because he did something a little, resentment, anger, I got confused.

Daria, Tyumen, 24 years old

Alyona:

Desha, judging by your letter, you showed the initiative in sex, not your man. How else to explain the fact that you "lost the prelude"? And your roommate has not been particularly zealous in diversifying your sex life before, and now he has completely withdrawn from this. I can only assume that you initially chose a man with a low sexual temperament as your partner, and the longer you live with him, the less you want to draw on your not very rich sex life. And yours the "husband" was just fine with the fact that the initiative in these matters came from you.

In my opinion, if everything is so dull after less than two years of living together, then it makes no sense to wait for sudden changes for the better. You are only 24 years old, and sex is one of the components of a young life. Let not the main one, but specifically with this partner you completely withered away. Yes, it happens that after many years of living together, spouses are no longer so active in bed, especially when family chores and caring for children are superimposed on the relationship of the two. But not at 24 and not a couple of years after we met. So I would have already thought about stopping this family experiment.

It doesn't bring you physical or emotional satisfaction. And besides, it's far from a fact that your common-law husband has not already found alternative ways to have fun. I have little faith in young men who don't need sex at all. If he does not receive it with you, he will find someone to satisfy his desires with. But, of course, this is not a reason to rape yourself in bed if a man does not excite you at all, and his lack of initiative generally annoys and causes anger and resentment. This is a reason to change partners. What is the point of toiling with him all his life until retirement?

Sergey:

Daria, I don't understand. How could "foreplay" be lost on your part if a man should do it? Or is it the other way around for you? It wasn't your husband who excited you and prepared you for sex, but you him? Then you have a strange relationship. Although, of course, how many people - so many opinions. As for the cooling of passion, then, alas, this is a completely natural phenomenon. Believe me, there is not a single family or couple created by mentally normal people where the sex life would not change over time. After all, we are all humans, not machines. And no matter how much we love our partner, no matter how much we want him physically at the beginning of a relationship, after a while the passion inevitably goes away. However, this does not mean at all that the feelings are gone. It's just time for a shift in priorities. And if earlier it seemed that sex is everything, now the understanding has come, that intimacy is just one of the components of family life. And it's far from the most important. And then, just believe me, it will be even more interesting.

After all, everyone's sexual temperament is different. Yes, and all sorts of physiological processes can leave their mark. And there are people who, for some reason, at one time or another generally lose the desire to have sex. For example, a woman breastfeeding a newborn baby. Therefore, what happens between you is completely natural and normal. You grow up, change, and desires and needs change accordingly. And sex in this regard is just a litmus test for more general processes. But, unfortunately, not always young people manage to painlessly survive the ongoing changes. It is very important how people treat each other, whether they are ready to compromise or to infringe on their own desires to please a partner. And if in fact there is no mutual understanding in a couple, just as there is no desire to jointly look for options for solving problems, then the situation will inevitably come to a standstill. And there will be a break. But I do not advise playing a tragedy on this occasion. No, it’s a pity, of course, for the lost time, and in general ... But if your boyfriend doesn’t understand your desires, if you can’t explain to him what you want, or he just doesn’t want to listen to it, then why continue this whole circus? After all, such crises are just what is needed so that young people learn to live together, begin to feel themselves as something in common and solve common problems. For in the future, the couple will have to take on the responsibilities of parents, which will inevitably entail changes in their personal lives.

As for your case, then you must admit that you do not want so much sex itself, as you are tired of its usual course. But what if your boyfriend just offers you to relax and have fun, and then brings you to orgasm, without demanding anything in return? It is unlikely that you will refuse this. Therefore, in your case, it is better to talk not about a decrease in desire, but about changes in relations with a young man, which, alas, are not going for the better. Can you change something? Theoretically, yes. You can, for example, talk frankly with a guy and talk about your own desires or reluctances. Will it help, I don't know. But as an option. Without asking for anything in return? It is unlikely that you will refuse this. Therefore, in your case, it is better to talk not about a decrease in desire, but about changes in relations with a young man, which, alas, are not going for the better. Can you change something? Theoretically, yes. You can, for example, talk frankly with a guy and talk about your own desires or reluctances. Will it help, I don't know. But as an option. Without asking for anything in return? It is unlikely that you will refuse this. Therefore, in your case, it is better to talk not about a decrease in desire, but about changes in relations with a young man, which, alas, are not going for the better. Can you change something? Theoretically, yes. You can, for example, talk frankly with a guy and talk about your own desires or reluctances. Will it help, I don't know. But as an option.

MYTH 2. A man always wants sex, but a woman is not very interested in it.

Even if you do not agree with this and know very well how things really are, try to convince most of the men, and even women, on planet Earth of the opposite. For too long, scientists have summed up various theories under supposedly natural frigidity. Women brought up by religious restrictions. A woman's sexuality is not as obvious as a man's, and it's not always easy to wake her up. Perhaps, indeed, most men feel bad without abstinence, and most women find it easy, in their youth, young men experience attraction more often, and girls basically only allow themselves to be seduced ... But one cannot say with certainty about each specific person what and how he will experience, one cannot expect his behavior inherent in the majority.

You might be surprised to know that not every man behaves like a rabbit, throwing himself at everyone and dreaming about sex every second. The image of a real macho is just one of the ideals of a man, which not everyone can match and which not everyone likes, but many try to follow this "ideal" in order to socialize in a society with such attitudes.

Generalizations are harmful if they prevent us

from accepting ourselves as we are created. You read that a female representative really wants sex only at 30-35, the peak of her sexuality. But you have the opposite, and at 17, hormones rage much more than at 35. If you forget about how different we are, you can start to have complexes and worry about whether you are normal, and whether you need to redo yourself, or start already reproach and hate yourself for being different from others.

In fact, the speed of puberty is individual for everyone. And it is not at all necessary for a woman to be cold as an iceberg, just because someone thinks so. And a man to be at the peak of his abilities every day. Everyone has a different sexual temperament, as experience, observations and statistics show.

Men may want sex once a week, a month, or two or three times a day. All options are within the normal range. The same goes for women. In youth, men have a greater temperament, as sexologists write, and women "bloom" in this sense after 30. The reality, as already mentioned, may be different. One man performs one sexual intercourse per night, but for an hour and a half, and the other - four or five for three minutes. And all these options are within the normal range.

Whether your temperaments match with your husband is an important point. If he needs sex every day, and once a week is enough for you, how long can you try to change your nature and force yourself, going against your desires? Will you look for an excuse to avoid sex time after time, or will you let your husband find a more temperamental lover? Is it not because of such situations that jokes are told about a wife who has a headache all the time? And vice versa: it's quite enough for a husband to "stick" to his wife once a month or a week, but she needs more often, dissatisfaction causes irritation and anger, she rolls up scandals and suspects her husband of treason ... It's hard for both, whatever one may say. Therefore, it is best to pay attention to this factor in advance, even before marriage. Even by courtship, you can understand how active partners are in terms of sex. And harmony in the family is largely associated with harmony in the intimate life of spouses, but how can a clear imbalance in needs be harmonious? Either this problem will snowball and cause separation, or one of the spouses will find solace outside the family. A forced measure for those who are so comfortable, who love each other, but can neither adjust nor get used to the difference in temperaments. Any solution to the problem is fine if it suits all family members and does not cause negativity in someone.

He only wants me twice a week

I would like to share with you the following problem. I have been living in a civil marriage for a year now. I love my young man very much. Everything about him suits me: kind, good, just super, the only BUT. We have different sexual appetites with him .He has enough sex once or twice a week, but for me this is not enough, I would like more. I have repeatedly spoken to him about this topic, he does not understand me, he says that he has enough for so much ... I can't change him, my conscience does not allow ... What can be changed in this situation? Is three or four times a week really unrealistic for a man? Or do everyone have different needs? Or maybe I don't understand something, or I demand something unrealistic? By the way, he is my first man, before him there was no sex with anyone.

Anfisa, St. Petersburg, 24 years old

Alyona:

Well, how is it going for you? Do you expect initiative from him? Or your initiative is suppressed by him? There can be so many reasons for refusing more frequent intimacy that it is better to discuss them with a specialist, and not in a circle of girlfriends and unfamiliar women. Maybe he is not inspired by the quality of sex, which is why he limits himself to one or two times a week. Maybe he gets tired at work, burns out and simply doesn't have enough strength to be active in bed these days, but he doesn't want to say this, for example, he's shy. Maybe there's something about you that doesn't suit him. The reasons are many. Have you tried taking matters into your own hands? How skillful and interesting are you as a lover? If a man is not impotent and feels sympathy for a woman, it is enough to try a little - and the desire will come. At least it's worth trying. And change on the basis that there is little sex and you need twice as much - this is stupid. Of course, if sex is not the only thing you live in this life.

Alternatively, talk to your boyfriend again, explain to him how important this is for you now. And ask him to satisfy you if he himself does not want anything. There are many other ways to do this. I hope at 24 years old they are already known.

Sergey:

We are all different people, and everyone's appetites too. In addition, I can assure you that with the passage of time and the increase in the time spent together, they will also decrease. True, much depends on your own desires and skills. In the end, almost any man can be bred for sex, even if he “well, I don’t want to at all.” Try to be more active in this matter. Take the process, or whatever else, into your own hands, so to speak. And go ahead. Where will he go from such a submarine? In general, all this is a grinding of characters. The main thing - do not be upset and do not invent anything superfluous on this topic. And it’s very easy to listen to friends and acquaintances, decide that if they don’t want to, then there is someone else, and destroy a wonderful relationship. I would very much like to wish that in your relations there will be disagreements only on this very correctable point.

If you want more sex, be active yourself.

It's hard for me without sex

I want to share with you my problem. Just don't judge too harshly. A year and a half ago, my husband left me, with whom we lived for eight years. We have a child. Two months later, I met a man to whom I became attached almost immediately, although I realized that we could not be together. I dated him for six months and then tried to break up with him for six months. The gap was given to me very hard, probably, there was a strong emotional attachment. Now I have been alone for five months and do not want a serious relationship with anyone. The problem is that without sex it is very difficult for me. But sex binds me, I start thinking constantly about a person, some kind of shame takes, I worry. I also can't just sleep with a stranger, I meet in terms of sex with people with whom I am in the same company (unmarried), and I don't give a damn about my reputation. It's just that the conscience torments and the feeling It seems stupid to me to start a hopeless relationship just for the sake of sex, but I can't change my attitude.

Marina, Moscow, 29 years old

Alyona:

I don't understand who is using whom. If you yourself are looking for sex in men, then After all, you are the "user", and they are the means to achieve your goals and satisfy your needs. That is exactly how you should think about it. Unless, of course, you date unmarried men only in search of sexual satisfaction. But I'm afraid your problem goes much deeper than that. No wonder you become attached to every partner you sleep with. It means that you are still tuned in to a more serious relationship, and when you are once again broken off, you begin to feel shame, the very thoughts "I was used for sex" appear in your head. Maybe it's time to admit to yourself that in fact, in every unmarried man from your environment, you see a potential partner for a normal relationship, but what happens is what happens: friendly sex without obligations. Do you know why? Because you set yourself up that way. Men, on the other hand, rarely seek to establish a serious relationship with women of your type. Sex is one thing, but a family needs one that does not have sexual desire in the first place. Analyze what you really want. You will be surprised.

Sergey:

Well, what can I say to you? You are an adult. Not bound by any moral obligations. And are you afraid to have sex? In my opinion, this is nonsense. With such problems, it is best to go to a psychologist. It seems to me personally that you just want a serious relationship and you are looking for them in every partner, but your partners just want sex. You know, maybe you should play sports? Here's my word of honor, after 40 minutes of intensive training on simulators, no sex is needed at all. Switch to something. After all, you are not a nymphomaniac. Try, just for fun, just take care of yourself. At least not for long. Well, in general, I do not know what to advise you. I hope that the forum members have a better idea of this situation and will be more useful than me. In any case, good luck and success.

If attraction has declined after a few years, and this causes grief for a husband and wife, there are several options to solve the problem:

– If the reason is fatigue from the monotony of family life, develop boredom with new experiences: a trip, a small joint vacation alone, experiments in bed, etc. If the reason is fatigue from the monotony of family life, develop boredom with new experiences - a trip, a small joint vacation alone, experiments in bed, etc.

– Check your health: the level of hormones in the blood, gynecological diseases, poor health affect the general condition, can cause depression, for which, at first glance, there is no reason. Nervous exhaustion, stress also affect intimate life.

– If you have too many worries, money problems, constant worry about raising children, etc., it is not surprising that you cannot simply relax and be alone with each other without taking all your panicky thoughts about the future to bed. You need the right environment, maybe some good wine, a nice movie or music... Recall what made you happy before!

Is it possible to live with a husband without sex?

I have been married for 11 years. My husband took care of me for 2.5 years, then we got married for love, we could no longer be apart. I was 22 and he was the first. Everything was fine, even small salaries did not spoil our relationship, we lived within our means. By the first date of their life together, there was a coolness in sex on his part. Then we had to move to live with his parents. A son and a daughter were born. They are now 5.5 and almost 4 years old. Three years ago we safely moved into our house. But we already live by inertia. I am sure that my husband has no one and never had. The lack of sex since the second year of marriage is freezing me. He says it's his nature. Over the past year, I'm ashamed to say, there were at most 10 moments of love. But he is only 35 years old. How much I cried from a feeling of humiliation that my own husband does not want me, young, beautiful, bright! After the birth of my daughter, I quickly recovered in figure, quit my unloved job and found a good position with a good salary. The men around did not hide their admiration. I have a lover. I justify myself by the fact that my health is deteriorating. I didn't want to leave my family and I don't want to. The husband does not guess or pretends. He treats me well, loves our children, helps with the housework and is always busy, mostly with men's affairs. We became partners in raising and raising children. Once I dropped this phrase, he was offended. And my lover goes crazy for me, asks to choose him, asks ... But I love children, and they love dad. I didn't want to leave my family and I don't want to. The husband does not guess or pretends. He treats me well, loves our children, helps with the housework and is always busy, mostly with men's affairs. We became partners in raising and raising children. Once I dropped this phrase, he was offended. And my lover goes crazy for me, asks to choose him, asks ... But I love children, and they love dad. I didn't want to leave my family and I don't want to. The husband does not guess or pretends. He treats me well, loves our children, helps with the housework and is always busy, mostly with men's affairs. We became partners in raising and raising children. Once I dropped this phrase, he was offended. And my lover goes crazy for me, asks to choose him, asks ... But I love children, and they love dad.

Anya, Russia, 33 years old

Alyona:

Anya, there is no sex for health. There are no diseases caused by the lack of sex (except for psychosomatic ones, which can arise even because your boss yelled at you). But there are sexually transmitted diseases. Especially if the sexual partner has to be shared with someone else, which in your case is more than likely. To justify your secret sexual pleasures by the fact that you need them to maintain a fragile female health is absurd. Tell this to the nuns and ascetics, who live no less than "mere mortals" and do not have sexual intercourse. It's not your "health" that needs sex, you need sex. It's in your head. For you, to be the object of male sexual desire means to be complete, to feel like a real woman. And this is your right. But if the need for self-expression through sex is so developed, then why did you live for so many years with a man who is not able to help you fulfill this need? On the other hand, what did you do for your part in order to arouse desire in your husband? For some reason, many people believe that after the wedding, sex becomes an obligatory part of the evening program, and they stop caring that some kind of romantic prelude precedes this evening action. That is, the husband and wife do nothing at all from what they did before the wedding, in order to end up in the same bed, passionately and hastily tearing off each other's clothes. And gradually sex becomes something every day and insipid, like brushing your teeth or scrambled eggs for breakfast. Meanwhile, sex is not only pleasure, it is also communication, and self-affirmation, and romance. And most importantly, sex is an expression of love. You and your husband used sex only as a tool for procreation. There is no love between you for a long time. You yourself write that sex came to naught in the first two years of marriage. At the same time, your eldest child is 5.5 years old. Why was it necessary to give birth in such circumstances? Have you looked for happiness in children? Did not find? Two children from an unloved husband, but an exemplary father - what's the point now to ask: "What to do?" Yes, kids love their dad. Yes, it would be a tragedy for them to find out that their mother wants to leave him. And waiting for them to grow up and understand everything is too long and practically useless. Now you will not envy your choice. A lover can be a good sex partner, but a bad stepfather for your children. The husband is a great father, but a useless lover. None of the solutions will bring you peace. Probably the best psychotherapist. Perhaps your decision will be beyond the two obvious (husband or lover).

Sergey:

Anya, in my opinion, should not be wishful thinking. You never truly loved each other. After all, sex, like many other things in the family, is a mutual matter. And it all depends on how people understand, appreciate and respect each other. Of course, we are all different and everyone has their own temperament, including sexual. However, if two people really love, then they can always find a compromise. All that is needed here is a common desire to understand and "appease" each other. And therefore, blaming only one side for the lack of sex or something else is completely wrong. This is a two way process. And if your husband does not want you, it means that you are not trying very hard for this either. In fact, this is true in reverse as well. Therefore, we have to state that you and your husband, although you have lived for 11 years, do not know and do not understand each other at all. Frankly, even strange how did you manage to live together for so long? In this regard, I think you did not marry for great love. Rather, your husband's long and persistent courtship simply went from quantity to quality.

Judging by the description, he is a thorough and persistent person. Only for you, with your love for yourself, so young, beautiful and bright, perseverance alone at the first stage was not enough. And while the husband could "keep up the mark", confirming your dignity, everything was fine. But as soon as life, habit and worries began to take their toll, as soon as the man was distracted and became himself, you immediately got bored and began to look for adventure. Yes, he's good too. Knowing the problem, doing nothing is a direct provocation of the growth of horns. That's what I got. Your husband's long and persistent courtship just went from quantity to quality. Judging by the description, he is a thorough and persistent person. Only for you, with your love for yourself, so young, beautiful and bright, perseverance alone at the first stage was not enough. And while the husband could "keep up the mark", confirming your dignity, everything was fine. But as soon as life, habit and worries began to take their toll, as soon as the man was distracted and became himself, you immediately got bored and began to look for adventure.

Yes, he's good too. Knowing the problem, doing nothing is a direct provocation of the growth of horns. That's what I got. Your husband's long and persistent courtship just went from quantity to quality. Judging by the description, he is a thorough and persistent person. Only for you, with your love for yourself, so young, beautiful and bright, perseverance alone at the first stage was not enough. And while the husband could "keep up the mark", confirming your dignity, everything was fine. But as soon as life, habit and worries began to take their toll, as soon as the man was distracted and became himself, you immediately got bored and began to look for adventure. Yes, he's good too. Knowing the problem, doing nothing is a direct provocation of the growth of horns. That's what I got. Perseverance alone was not enough at the first stage. And while the husband could "keep up the mark", confirming your dignity, everything was fine. But as soon as life, habit and worries began to take their toll, as soon as the man was distracted and became himself, you immediately got bored and began to look for adventure. Yes, he's good too. Knowing the problem, doing nothing is a direct provocation of the growth of horns. That's what I got. Perseverance alone was not enough at the first stage. And while the husband could "keep up the mark", confirming your dignity, everything was fine. But as soon as life, habit and worries began to take their toll, as soon as the man was distracted and became himself, you immediately got bored and began to look for adventure. Yes, he's good too. Knowing the problem, doing nothing is a direct provocation of the growth of horns. That's what I got.

Only now I'm sure that you are also very "horned", you just don't notice it. In this regard, there are probably two options. The first is divorce. And secondly, you don’t need to change anything yet. You have a family, you live together and are not going to run away. This is good. And the fact that everyone has a “left secret” only unites them even more. After all, guilt in front of a partner and children does not allow you to disperse. And will not give in the future. And if so, then what difference does it make who you have sex with? No, it would be safer, of course, to get a dildo and masturbate. But if this is disgusting, and the rest is acceptable in principle, then advice to you and love. The main thing is that your lovers do not start to show excessive initiative. For as long as the "left" life is, as it were, hidden, you can keep living together. However, if all this suddenly comes out, you will have to get a divorce.

Chapter 2

A lady, a real lady, couldn't look people in the eye after a night like this. But over the feeling of shame triumphed the memory of pleasure, of the ecstasy that seized her when she yielded to his caresses. For the first time she felt that she was living life to the fullest, she felt a passion as all-encompassing and primal as the fear that had possessed her that night when she had fled from Atlanta, as dizzyingly sweet as the cold hatred with which she had shot that Yankee.

Margaret Mitchell. Gone With the Wind

Surely you have heard more than once or twice that a woman is fabulously lucky. This is a man who experiences only one orgasm in one sexual intercourse and only one kind (although, strictly speaking, homosexuals can actually argue with this, but we are still talking about the female sex), and a woman can have more than one in an hour, and a few orgasms, and even a few different sensations. But on the other hand, it's enough for a man to achieve an orgasm easy, because for him this is primarily a matter of physiology, but we need a combination of several factors.

Yes, ideally, a woman is able to experience all types of orgasm, but many note that they manage to feel only clitoral or exclusively vaginal in their life. The sensitivity of different erogenous zones is not the same for everyone, and we follow the usual path: having once experienced a certain kind of pleasure, we continue to achieve it and put an end to trying to achieve something else. The natural sensitivity of the body, as well as the perception of pain, can be increased and decreased initially, but it is possible to expand the scope of pleasure by trying new things and listening to yourself.

Clitoral orgasm - the most common and easily achievable type of pleasure, the source of which is the organ of the body, which is responsible precisely for the woman to enjoy during the conception of children. And his mechanical irritation - while riding a bicycle, uncomfortable posture, tight clothing - can also lead to orgasm, and many quickly learn to remove the general excitement by masturbation, which involves a very accessible clitoris. However, women who have not masturbated prior to sexual intercourse are unfamiliar with the clitoral orgasm and where one of the sources of pleasure is located. If a man is also a beginner in these matters, this "useful little thing" is forgotten, and they cannot be found. During intercourse, the clitoris is not directly affected, at least not in all positions, and therefore a woman accustomed to a clitoral orgasm, during foreplay, a man can give as much attention as possible to the entire clitoral area, and the woman will be truly satisfied.

What means will help in this situation? First, there are positions where the clitoris is more exposed: sitting face to face, for example. Secondly, why not help yourself with your free hand right during intercourse?

Thirdly, a man can also contribute with his hand in the process. Well, during foreplay, a man can pay as much attention as possible to the entire area of the clitoris, and the woman will be truly satisfied. True, the help of a man does not always leave a satisfied woman. Since he does not have a clitoris, he does not know exactly what and how to do, plus the sensitivity of this organ is different for everyone. And it is difficult to please a woman: while caressing herself, she focuses on her feelings, and a man must be able to respond to her sighs and manifestations of emotions. And if you shrink and, in embarrassment, do not show your reaction in any way, how can a man determine does he do everything right, or is it at this very second that he acts too slowly or too gently on your "pleasure center"? No way! Moreover, for him it becomes a boring task, because for him the most interesting thing in such caresses is to give you pleasure and make sure that he managed to do it in the best possible way. If you do not show, do not teach him how to caress your unique body, but will simulate an orgasm, so long as these attempts of his end, you will cheat yourself.

If you do not show, do not teach him how to caress your unique body, but will simulate an orgasm, so long as these attempts of his end, you will cheat yourself.

Attempts to describe the difference between orgasms usually have one thing in common: pleasure starts from one specific area of the body and expands to cover the entire body. The difference between orgasms is conditional, they can mix with each other, differ in intensity. Of particular importance - what kind of orgasm you experience - no, it would be nice for you. Diversity is interesting, but getting upset about what you didn't feel some other kind of orgasm, not worth it. True, you can try to focus on the sensations in that particular area of the body that usually does not cause you an orgasm, although it can theoretically, and catch the pleasant that the impact on this area of the body reveals to you.

Vaginal orgasm - occurs during exposure to the vagina. The G-spot that is talked about so much is not a magic button, it is not necessary for a man to find it in order to please a woman, because during intercourse it will be found automatically. Pay attention to what is felt in that very area during intercourse, feel all the nuances, imagine that the heat covers the vaginal area, as if it were a clitoral orgasm that has shifted in depth. Experiment with frictions, direction, strength, speed, try different poses. Each woman has her own body structure, the length and location of the vagina, and it depends on these nuances which position will be more pleasant, which one is more convenient, etc. Yes, by the way, a lot also depends on the size of a man's dignity. The better the match between the thickness of the penis and the vagina, the easier it is to achieve a vaginal orgasm.

The longer the PMU (male penis), the easier it is to reach the cervix during friction, and if it is open - which happens when the woman is maximally aroused and not tight - the pleasure will be special (and, keep in mind, the chances of conception are higher). This is the so-called uterine orgasm. There are positions that promote maximum penis penetration, even if it is not that big.

Too long for the parameters of a particular woman, the MUF, on the contrary, causes discomfort and limits some postures. And delivering oral sex to a man with a giant penis is much more difficult. So the main thing is not the size, but the coincidence of the physiological parameters of a man and a woman. Well, the ability to use what nature has given.

The main thing is not the size, but the coincidence of the physiological parameters of a man and a woman. The vaginal orgasm is described as more all-encompassing, and the clitoral orgasm is described as more localized, but all this is individual.

During anal sex, a woman receives another type of orgasm - anal. "There" also has nerve endings, the sensations are special and have their own characteristic features. If you don't enjoy this kind of sex at all, or give it up so as not to suffer, or practice relaxing, ask your husband to be more careful and gentle, guide him yourself and don't forget about the lubricant that is sold in any pharmacy and facilitates penetration wherever whatever it was and slip. In order not to harm your health, it is better to practice sex of this kind infrequently, but the less often it is, the more pleasure it will bring to both, like a rare exotic that brings variety, like a holiday that would get bored if it came daily.

Finally, for some women, even a long kiss, dance, caress in the chest, neck area causes an orgasm - and each option brings her incomparable pleasure with anything else. And no less than with other types of orgasm, that is, it also has a period of growth, peak and completion. This orgasm is called extra genital m. No wonder there are meditative practices of tantric sex. Perhaps all its conventions and rules will seem too complicated and boring for you and your partner, but some of them will definitely come in handy for you. The fact is that with proper attention to each other, the desire to give pleasure and at the same time to know new sensations, you can explore your bodies from the point of view of pleasure and discover many new things. What can become an erogenous zone?

Anything: palm, elbow bend, inner thighs, base of the neck, etc. Much depends on the intensity of caresses: a light touch of a feather, light pressure, biting, scratching someone likes only one of the above, and someone responds to different days for different effects. Our fingers, tongue are great tools of love, and you can also influence with your voice, sighs, groans, whisper affectionate words or dirty curses - whatever you like, use pieces of ice or sweet and skin-cooling cream or a type of lubricant that causes non-illusory heat.

Perhaps it would be worth adding here the emotional orgasm that we experience when we listen to especially touching music, look at a particularly beautiful landscape, go swimming, experience emotional stress ... Sensuality is a kind of fusion of events and moods, and therefore it is so important for a woman to do not just sex but love. Sensuality is a kind of fusion of events and moods, and therefore it is so important for a woman to engage not just in sex, but in love.

To achieve an orgasm, sometimes it is enough to hear from a loved one a stream of compliments, confessions, words of admiration or frank and detailed descriptions of what he wants to do with you that night. So the question "Is it possible to achieve orgasm without touching?" may be considered closed. This is real. Try and bring your man to such pleasure by non-standard means.

Why is it that we don't get it all that often in reality? What's stopping you? Firstly, you need to love each other very much in order to want to deliver all these joys not only to yourself, but also to your partner. It is much easier to act in the usual way, without wasting time and - most importantly - effort on all these delights. And we need, as you understand, an initiative from both sides.

You can talk a lot about why it is sometimes so difficult to achieve an orgasm with a man: the wrong environment, spoiled by something mood, extraneous thoughts, inability to relax, distrust of a man, feeling unwell and much more. There are sad statistics that say that some women do not experience orgasm at all.

Excitation does not end with an explosion of sensations, there is no growing pleasure that has a peak point and ends with complete relaxation. If there is excitement, then it is possible to find a way out for it.

The epigraph to this chapter is a quote from a classic work, dedicated to how a woman sometimes reveals herself unexpectedly even for herself. It may take years before she reveals her sensuality. But perhaps it is much earlier, from the very beginning. What does it take to experience an orgasm other than the effort of a loving man? If there is excitement, then it is possible to find a way out for it. If there is no reaction at all to the actions of a man, this needs to be resolved with a psychologist: childhood trauma, body characteristics, not that man? If there is, you need to look at what prevents you from reaching the logical end. Most often, it is a psychological barrier in the head, due to the fact that a woman cannot relax and get distracted from everything else, do not think about how she looks, what her partner will think about her behavior, etc. The ability to relax is an important quality, light meditations to train this feature can help.

There are various psychological reasons for the inability to discard everything extraneous and trust a man. There are also reasons for dislike for her body, which prevent a woman from comprehending its secrets, its features, erogenous zones, listening to her feelings and admiring her, even if it is imperfect. Without self-love, it's hard to have a million orgasms a minute, honestly. The role of men in this is great, but not as much as the role of the woman herself. Without self-love, it's hard to have a million orgasms a minute, honestly. The role of men in this is great, but not as much as the role of the woman herself. Without self-love, it's hard to have a million orgasms a minute, honestly.

The role of men in this is great, but not as much as the role of the woman herself. Relax and have fun - this is just one of hundreds of leisure activities such as sex. Passivity is not very useful here. Your orgasm is largely in your hands: your mood, your initiative, your body movements and interest in the process will bring you mutual pleasure. Each sex can be an adventure if it is varied, if not afraid, but simply to please each other in new ways, returning to the tried and true from time to time. Your orgasm is largely in your hands: your mood, your initiative, your body movements and interest in the process will bring you mutual pleasure.

I live with my husband as with a brother

My husband and I have been together for eight years. There is a daughter, 1.5 years old. The husband works, carries everything into the house, does not smoke, and drinks sometimes. Everything would be fine, but I look at him and understand that there is no more that love, he is a dear and dear person to me, but we live like brother and sister, in every sense. I'm tired of taking everything on myself. The house is on me, the child is on me, but from my husband there is no affection, no love, and no warmth. I loved him madly, for his sake I switched to part-time and moved to another country. And now I feel nothing, only emptiness. Maybe it's a crisis, maybe it's the end. He is my first man, the first one I started dating seriously, nine years older than me. I want to live, to enjoy life, not to exist. I thought that for the sake of my daughter I should save and try to restore everything, but I understand that I don't want and I can't. There is no one on the side. I just want a new relationship but I can't destroy my family because of my desires. I'm at a dead end.

Karina, USA, 26 years old

Alyona:

Karina, this is not a crisis, this is a typical fatigue of a young mother, locked in four walls with her baby. Your daughter is only one and a half years old, which means that you spent these one and a half years at home, taking care of a small child. Hence the stagnation in the head, and thoughts about fatigue, crisis and so on. The first one and a half to two years with a baby are the most difficult. Especially if there are no nannies or grandmothers who would take on some of the worries, so that you have time for yourself and your personal interests. But I wouldn't blame my husband for not "helping" you with the baby and around the house. In your family, responsibilities are clearly distributed: the husband works, providing for the family economically, and, as you yourself write, “Carries everything into the house.” You, accordingly, provide “rear”: you look after the house and the child. This is a completely standard distribution of duties, and just trust me, few husbands and wives manage to visit each other's place in order to understand that both “works” require strength and exhaust them both physically and mentally by the end of the day. And as a result, the husband, who comes home from work tired, does not understand why the wife is waiting for him to help around the house and tries to give him the child. And the wife is offended that her husband, who was absent from home all day, does not want to take care of the child and help around the house. One is perplexed: “You have been sitting at home all day.” Second: “You were not at home all day ...” does not want to take care of the child and help around the house. One is perplexed: "You've been sitting at home all day." Second: “You were not at home all day ...” does not want to take care of the child and help around the house. One is perplexed: "You've been sitting at home all day." Second: “You were not at home all day ...”

I was probably lucky that, by coincidence, my husband and I had to change places and roles, so both I and he are well aware of the inconsistency of such claims from one side and the other. Try and you look at your situation from different angles. Husband works, so do you. Each of you has your own front of work. If you need his help, can you ask him for it? You can also discuss the fact that for a year and a half you are already tired of the monotonous life in four walls with a baby. Perhaps the husband does not realize that you are fed up with your "happiness of motherhood." After all, for sure the child is desired, and, therefore, for him your present life this is what you dreamed of. Are you silent? Even after 20 years of marriage, people do not become telepaths. So a dialogue on this topic is simply vital for your couple. Maybe you need a nanny to help you with the baby or so that you can resume work (if you worked before pregnancy). In addition, the older your daughter is, the more opportunities your family will have for interesting joint leisure.

Vacation trips, for example. In general, do not rush to far-reaching conclusions. Your family is experiencing natural growth difficulties due to the arrival of a small child, on whom you are both dependent and to whom your life is now subordinate. The baby will grow up - it will become easier, you will become more mobile, your free evenings and days will be more diverse. But, I repeat, what you are experiencing now, you must definitely discuss with your husband. Not in the form of "you have become a stranger" or "I'm tired of pulling the house and my daughter on myself", but in the form of "I need your support and help, I'm tired, but I really want to enjoy life again ..."

Sergey:

Karina, in my opinion, before embarking on a free voyage in a foreign country, and even with a small child in her arms, it is worth thinking over everything very well more than once or even twice. Now you have a house, you have a husband who provides for you, but what will happen if you leave? And where are you going to go? Or do you already have another lover in mind, ready to accept both you and the child? But even in this case, you should think carefully, because it is one thing to declare intentions and quite another put them into practice. To leave your husband, you yourself need to be very firmly on your feet, have a steady income and a place to live. Otherwise, you may find yourself sitting firmly on the beans, without support and even without a child. Therefore, for starters, if you are tired of dragging the house and the child on yourself, you should at least talk about it with your husband. After all, when a person wants affection, love and warmth, he means very specific actions on the part of others. So tell your spouse about them. I don't think that the person with whom you lived for eight years, and lived, apparently, not in the worst possible way, will not want to at least talk. You can't figure it out yourself - go to a family psychologist, fortunately in America there are no problems with this. Then find a job, learn how to earn money yourself.

Alas, very often people experience such mental anguish, who do not even imagine what it is to work and earn money, and therefore simply do not understand the feelings and sensations of a partner coming home from work. So go to work. After that, if you still can't figure it out with your husband, contact lawyers and carefully prepare for a divorce. And only then seriously think about breaking up the relationship. However, first, nevertheless, try to solve the matter peacefully and start with yourself. After all, believe me, the joy of life she is not in her husband and not in money. She's in the head. And in yours. And if YOU suddenly lost joy, then start with YOURSELF. Find a job, some hobby, YOURSELF stop living only at home and with a child. Then the world around will change, and the husband, quite possibly, will look at you differently.

Why do you even need an orgasm? Often in books and articles on this subject it is reported that it is not necessary for a woman to reach an orgasm every time, there is nothing wrong with the fact that during sex, before or after there was no explosion of pleasure. Yes, of course, there is no need to complex about this. I just want tenderness, and there is no need for vivid sensations today - so be it. But if you really want to, if the excitement was great, but no discharge came? The husband was too hasty, you were tense, or suddenly distracted by a loud sound outside the window ... If there was a very strong excitement, it will not disappear, it, like ball lightning, will wander in the body, demanding discharge, threatening to pour out tears, a scandal - anything, only to get rid of the painful tension. If there is no satisfaction from intimate life for a long time, this tension accumulates and threatens the woman with stress, a nervous breakdown. You can learn to direct all your energy to creativity, work, etc., just as monks put their energy into prayer, but the sexual area of life must also find its embodiment. If there has been no satisfaction from intimate life for a long time, this tension accumulates and threatens the woman with stress, a nervous breakdown.

If there is a husband nearby, if there is no need to be in asceticism, but the orgasm still does not occur, if the stomach aches after sex, you want to cry, heaviness in your soul ... Do you remember the quote from the Soviet book that was distributed on Runet: should let her go to the bathroom, but don't follow her, let her be alone. Maybe she wants to cry..."? This means that the orgasm has not come, and this causes discomfort. But the husband can help to avoid them: after intercourse, noticing your condition, caress with your hands, tongue, affectionate word ... Sometimes five minutes of attention after sex is enough to bring a woman to a happy outcome. And if everything worked out, the woman will cry with pleasure, she will feel light and at the same time weakness will come, she will want to lie in bed again, which is another instinct, related to reproduction: so that the seed does not spill out, this same instinct makes a woman rest for a few minutes after successful sex. Well, after a real orgasm, and even more than one in a row, after a while you jump up and feel able to move mountains, a happy smile does not leave your face, in general - you can wish everyone to experience such pleasure not too rarely, but rather more often.

I don't like the woman in me

I can’t establish a personal life, because I don’t feel like a woman. Men don't pay attention to me. Women's outfits, cosmetics are alien to me ... It's a pity to spend money on all this. But even if it's free, I don't deserve all this. The choice of cosmetics is hard labor. Since childhood (parents divorced), I didn’t see that a woman can be unconditionally loved, I think that love needs to be “earned”. Women who put on make-up are slaves of cosmetics, it is no longer possible to go out without makeup, and besides, they quickly age terribly ugly. I'm like a man in a skirt, even men's thoughts are analytical and pragmatic, without romance. Please help me to change and tell me how to help my inner woman to be realized and be happy. Thanks in advance!

Olga, St. Petersburg, 24 years old

Alyona:

Olay, all the clichés you listed about women are an attempt to justify your own laziness in regard to caring for your own appearance. Men do not pay attention to groomed, slovenly women. They have no interest in women who do not care about themselves, who are not interested in themselves. And that's exactly what you're doing. Women who use cosmetics do not age "horribly and quickly." In order for this to happen, a specific lifestyle must be added to cheap decorative cosmetics. And the daily use of good care cosmetics, combined with high-quality decorative ones, on the contrary, will prolong the youthfulness of your skin. For example, if you have not just a cream for the skin around the eyes, but a cream with UV protection. Not just a toner that evens out the complexion, but a toner with a complex of antioxidants ... And only those who can't paint at all. Why focus on such in your idea of femininity? You judge with clichés because it's so convenient for you. This can cover up your complete ignorance in the field of cosmetics for women, without bothering to study this issue. Grapes are green because they hang high. Start studying this topic not by the painted faces of prostitutes on Nevsky Prospect (or where do they go out there in masse?). You don't even have to embarrass yourself in front of anyone for this: YouTube is now full of good video courses on facial skin care and applying discreet everyday makeup.

Without bothering to study this issue. Grapes are green because they hang high. Start studying this topic not by the painted faces of prostitutes on Nevsky Prospect (or where do they go out there en masse?). You don't even have to embarrass yourself in front of anyone for this: YouTube is now full of good video courses on facial skin care and applying discreet everyday makeup. Without bothering to study this issue. Grapes are green because they hang high. Start studying this topic not by the painted faces of prostitutes on Nevsky Prospect (or where do they go out there end masse?). You don't even have to embarrass yourself in front of anyone for this: YouTube is now full of good video courses on facial skin care and applying discreet everyday makeup.

The same applies to clothing. To buy beautiful clothes for yourself, it's not enough just to understand it and have the funds for it. First of all, you need to love yourself. To love that very "inner woman" that you write about in your question. To love and pamper like a mother pampers a child. And learn to admire the result of this pampering. Your mother, of course, did you a disservice by outweighing all her complexes and stereotypes on your young head. Love cannot be earned. But you can't get it for nothing, because in order to be loved, you must like yourself. And this is the main

"Work". And you are too lazy to spend time and money on yourself. Perhaps, in your case, the best way out of the situation is to undergo personal growth training or something similar. Such classes are good for straightening the brain and get rid of the patterns and clichés inherited from narrow-minded parents. Olay, you are only 24 years old, stop thinking like an old woman who left her youth in the middle of the last century, when dust and hydroperite were in use, and stylish clothes were a sign of "licentiousness". Your mom is unlucky in life. But this is her personal life. She did not have time to simply love you and instill in you an interest and love for your own "I". So, this is your most important task for the near future.

Sergey:

Olga, such problems are not solved in Internet correspondence. This requires quite painstaking and not particularly pleasant work on oneself. And it is better to conduct it under the guidance of specialists and, in my opinion, in a group. The most important thing is that you already have the desire to change. You already feel that you are not right in your own views, and you want to change them. However, it is not so easy to independently give up everything that is acquired by unbearable self-flagellation. Therefore, I believe that in your case, the most correct way out would be to choose such a psychological group for yourself as soon as possible, since there are no problems in this regard in St. Petersburg. Then, if everything goes well, you yourself will feel the desire to spend money on yourself. As for your opinion that women who put on make-up are slaves of cosmetics, as well as everything else, then all this is nothing more than a manifestation of your inferiority complex, from which you just want to get rid of. And therefore, as soon as your self-esteem changes, these thoughts will also undergo changes.

To experience the pleasure of sex, you need to love yourself, your body and accept things that may initially seem difficult to understand. Overcome modesty, get used to the male body, to the peculiarities of sexual intercourse, learn to use your body and study it. And all this is much easier with a loving and beloved man. It is not so important whether you are experienced or not, how important is attention to each other. To be able to feel whether a partner is good or not, to correct actions in time, to have a desire to please him and to know that you will get the same from him, that he will not laugh at you in an intimate moment, will not be horrified by something, but will try to understand you and will accept anyone ... All this is love, or at least mutual respect, without which it will be difficult to fully open up in sex.

To experience the pleasure of sex, you need to love yourself, your body and accept things that may initially seem difficult to understand. Experiments in bed require preparation - theoretical and psychological. It is important to know that your proposal will not be rejected abruptly, that the partner will study the issue and try to share with you what he can. But, of course, violence is unacceptable here, so the psychological rejection of some kind of affection is also a reason to refuse it to a partner. Maybe not right away, but later you will try that too.

Shocked by anal sex

We have been married for a year, our relationship is harmonious, and we love each other very much and believe that we are the perfect couple. In bed, too, complete harmony. The problem is this. Once my husband offered me anal sex. I have always been negative about it. I know that before me he had experience and he liked it. In the end, he persuaded me. The experiment, of course, failed. To say that I didn't like it is to say nothing. This caused in me SUCH a storm of the most disgusting and disgusting feelings. Both moral and physical. My husband, of course, reassured me, saying that he would NEVER ask for it again. But it became my nightmare, I think all the time about how vile, disgusting, unnatural it is. These thoughts infuriate me, I don't want to think about it, but they themselves climb into my head. I, like a fool, look for articles about this, read them and rage, and then comment on this bestiality to my husband. He himself has long believed that it is sinful and vile. I know that he will never ask me for this, but I cannot calm down, I hate all the people on the planet who do this.

I understand that it is stupid to torment yourself with this. But I'm ready to lead the movement against it. My husband laughs at me, calls me stupid. Just don't say that anal is normal and whoever wants to, let him do it, I have already read a lot about this. Considering this the norm is the same as considering pedophilia or BDSM as the norm, but that's another topic. Help me get rid of the thoughts that prevent me from living a normal life. What a stupid thing to do to yourself. But I'm ready to lead the movement against it. My husband laughs at me, calls me stupid. Just don't say that anal is normal and whoever wants to, let him do it, I have already read a lot about this. Considering this the norm is the same as considering pedophilia or BDSM as the norm, but that's another topic. Help me get rid of the thoughts that prevent me from living a normal life. What a stupid thing to do to yourself. But I'm ready to lead the movement against it. My husband laughs at me, calls me stupid. Just don't say that anal is normal and whoever wants to, let him do it, I have already read a lot about this. Considering this the norm is the same as considering pedophilia or BDSM as the norm, but that's another topic. Help me get rid of the thoughts that prevent me from living a normal life.

Olga, Ufa, Republic of Bashkiria, 26 years old

Alyona:

It reminds me of the behavior of a young girl from the times of the USSR, who, contrary to public opinion, agreed to have sexual intercourse with a man in the hope that it would be pleasant, but received nothing but pain and loss of virginity, and now she sits disappointed and angry at the whole world, ready to go to a monastery, because sex before marriage is sinful and low, and to think otherwise is debauchery and blasphemy.

How to get rid of an obsessive idea? Well, for example, to rewrite the ending of this story in your mind. Imagine for a moment that you like it. I know I'm asking for the impossible, but for your own good, try to imagine that the experience of anal sex with your husband was pleasurable. Would you then arrange excavations on the Internet, study this topic in more detail, get angry and worry? Of course not. You would treat it as another experience, nothing more. The problem is not that it happened in your life, but that you didn't like it and caused physical pain. Like the loss of virginity with an inept and insensitive partner, when there are no positive emotions left. Actually, in a sense, this is also a "loss of innocence", only from the other end. But it's already happened, right? Another in your place would draw conclusions and live on. And your obsession with this unpleasant event, frankly, draws on an obsessive-compulsive disorder, and this is no longer here, but to a specialist. I'm serious.

From myself, I can recommend the following: if everything is so running and you really can't switch to something else, do it forcibly. As soon as there is a desire to get into the Internet for the next portion of this nonsense, or it climbs into your head on its own, learn poetry. Just take any verse from any author and start cramming until you learn it. When the brain solves memory tasks, it has no time to be distracted, otherwise it will not be able to remember anything. And do it constantly. Take, for example, a volume of Nikolai Gumilyov and learn everything. Just do it with zeal for any attempt by your subconscious mind to spoil your mood again with stupid thoughts about anal sex. And you will enrich the spiritual world, and you will join the beautiful, and then there will be a reaction - every time nonsense gets into your head, you will read beautiful poems. Everything is better and more useful, than to sit on sites and read about anal sex, and then discuss all this with my husband. Nothing else to do? Here, take your head beautiful.

Sergey:

Personally, I just don't have time for such loops. I

get up quite early because I have to do pull-ups, walk the domestic cattle, wash, and feed, get myself together and run to repay my native organization in exchange for several bank notes at the end of the month. On the way, you need to listen and read another English lesson. I work from 9 am to 6 pm. Then I fly home like a bullet, because there are a lot of things that no one else will do but me, a little daughter with whom I need to talk, thereby giving my wife a little rest, then a quick sleep - and all over again. I strongly advise you to find something for yourself, at least some. Believe me, when your head is occupied with worries about the essentials, and your hands are busy with business, it simply won't work to get stuck on someone unpleasant event. You are looking for articles because, in my opinion, that there is simply nothing else to do. Go to work. Start learning some language. If both work and worries are present, but thoughts do not go away and interfere with life, then there is only one option - running to specialists. This is either a neurosis on the whole head - and then you need to deal with psychologists, or, much worse, a serious mental illness, with which psychiatry should already work.

There are specific desires and ways to satisfy them. Therefore, it is so important to understand the characteristics of your body, to find out what you need to achieve orgasm. Then you will look for a suitable partner for you who will satisfy your unconventional needs. We have already talked about physical parameters, about the conformity of temperaments, and there is also the possibility of an imbalance in the level of aggression in sex.

Another type of orgasm can be noted - an orgasm from violence. Every person has a different need for violence. From complete rejection of aggression in intimate life to BDSM with all the attributes. The tendency to aggression in sex cannot be recognized as something sharply negative if it does not harm others, but one must understand that harmony is also needed in this area. If you are strongly opposed and only accept soft caresses, and a man wants to strangle you lightly at the moment of orgasm, you will not be able to coexist together, because you will be afraid of this and understand that you do not fully satisfy your husband's needs if you refuse him this sexual game . And vice versa: you need a whip, and your husband is against it and finds it funny - you will obviously lack something in the relationship. So what are you going to do? Look for someone on the side, and it's inevitable.

Human nature is complex, and much of it is intertwined in such a way that it is difficult to separate one from the other. The pleasure of punishment, the game of rape, the pleasure of self-pity comes from the depths of our "I", from distant ancestors. This pleasure is special, and so strong that it is caused, among other things, by the strongest emotions: an alloy of fear, humiliation, helplessness, children's feelings of dependence on an adult, and much more that is individual and intimate. Even modest women sometimes want to pretend that they were tied to a bed and deprived of their freedom of choice, to succumb completely to someone else's power, and men - even very loving ones - sometimes passionately want to throw their woman on the table and, despite her screams and resistance, bring them to exhaustion without any forewords. However, there is a difference between real violence and pretending to get spicy and unusual pleasure: the ability to stop if the partner asks for it seriously. Even complex sadomasochistic games always involve an exit point, a key "EXIT", the presence of stop words (partners agree in advance which word will mean a desire to stop the game).

Is it worth it to self-flagellate if you like hard sex? No. Find someone who is happy to share these desires with you. And accept yourself for who you are. If no one suffers from your habits, then everything is fine.

Why is it better to find out all these nuances with a partner in advance? Because otherwise he may refuse relationships with shades that he does not accept. It is a pity that not everyone immediately understands this, and also does not immediately reveal to each other all their secrets. Mysteriousness is mysteriousness, and some things are better to say out loud right away, to discuss - not immediately talking about yourself, but simply at least discussing hypothetically, as it happens with others ... And understand the attitude to this from someone with whom you are just starting to meet. I know examples of how a woman was terribly disappointed by the betrayal of her husband, who suddenly left her and their little child after three years of marriage. He could not explain anything, except that it became difficult for him to understand her. It suddenly turned out that he did not like her music, and her interests, etc. And no wonder, of course, because she showed a clear tendency to masochism and she was delighted with everything unusual, but it seemed to her that all this was interesting to him too. Fortunately, you can be unusual and meet the same, and this woman managed to find a man who shared her passions.

I tend to be sadomasochistic...

Please help me to understand the following situation. I am 26 years old, not married (in general, there is no strong desire yet). There is a sexual partner (he is married), with whom I discovered a penchant for BDSM. The worst thing is that this need is progressing. Ordinary sex is no longer enough for me, and there are more and more bruises on my body. I myself ask a man about it, sometimes I don't even control the situation. I don't know what it could lead to. I can only see the result - mutual satisfaction from sex and the gratitude of a man for such a "feature" of mine. Perhaps in the future it will be difficult for me to find the right man to create a family that shares such a passion. And, perhaps, by this I narrow the circle of suitable candidates. So this worries me a little. Change in the family is unacceptable or undesirable for me. I know that a lot comes from childhood, but there I was never beaten, unlike my younger brother (he was given me as an example). I'm just wondering: where does this come from and is it necessary to start "sounding the alarm" already? Thank you in advance.

Natalia, Moscow, 26 years old

Alyona:

You know, I think as long as sadomasochistic motives are the main thing for you in relationships with men, you should not think about family at all. It will hardly be possible to call a normal family in which such relationships dominate. And to assume that a person prone to sadism in sex with a woman he loves will be an accommodating family man who goes to the store for bread, takes out the trash, raises children ... How do you imagine a husband who will bruise you during sex, and then go do homework with your daughter? So I would not advise looking for a husband with sadistic inclinations. What turns on and excites in sex can be a big problem in everyday family life. And in relations with children, how such a man will filter his inclinations is generally a problem! You won't deny that sadism is actually a pathology of the individual, and not a harmless one. If masochism harms only the subject himself, then sadism is aggression directed outward. So what about a family with such a man - you got excited.

Where does the tendency to masochism come from? Everyone has their own way. Sometimes one childhood impression is enough to form a certain secret need. Alfred Adler has a theory that the earliest childhood impressions leave an indelible mark on the individual. God knows what you might have seen and heard at a tender age. Many believe that masochism is associated with aggression in the family (punishment, etc.). This is not true.

Sergey:

In fact, as far as I know, such deviations of sexual behavior are popularly called perversions and, from the point of view of an ordinary layman, they need treatment. Moreover, in the Bible, if I don't confuse anything, it is written that for such antics of local residents, angels completely burned down as many as two cities. This I mean that the Lord God, apparently, is also not enthusiastic about all sorts of perversions. But, you see, who cares about this nowadays? Why certain deviations occur and how to deal with them, in my personal opinion, should be clarified with specialists. Therefore, since you yourself understand that something wrong is happening and it is progressing, but it scares you, then you should turn to psychologists. We certainly can't help here. We will only confuse even more and, perhaps, harm with our specific advice. You can start by reading the materials on masochism available on the Web. After all, it is this side of BDSM that attracts you. Read, analyze, and think. There are quite a few opinions on this. Official psychology refers masochism to psychopathology and describes many different variants of this phenomenon. Which one is yours, I don't know. In my personal opinion, anything is acceptable in a couple if it suits both partners and does not lead to contradictions with the Criminal Code. But if addiction occurs, and even more so when it starts to interfere or “strain”, you should contact specialists. if it suits both partners and does not lead to contradictions with the Criminal Code. But if addiction occurs, and even more so when it starts to interfere or “strain”, you should contact specialists. If it suits both partners and does not lead to contradictions with the Criminal Code. But if addiction occurs, and even more so when it starts to interfere or “strain”, you should contact specialists.

Let's add a comment to this letter, published on the Cleo website, since the author of the comment is clearly "in the know":

"Natalia! In my humble opinion, the main problem that is described in your letter is the following: you consider yourself not quite normal and are afraid that this will prevent you from building a family in the future. You are NOT abnormal. There are quite a lot of such people, and at the moment they have ceased to be afraid and have come out of the underground. Type in "Yandel" BDSM - they have their own clubs, forums, sites.

Following from this, you cannot be afraid that you will not find a mate))

And from life: as a rule, if such pairs of "sadist -

masochist" are created, then they have a very strong relationship. Perhaps more complex than those of people with ordinary sex addictions, but strong. As far as I know, BDSM implies a more trusting relationship between partners than in simple sex options.

Fanerka, DOK, Uryupinsk, Russia

To accept and understand yourself, you need to go through some experience, compare sensations, situations, and if one thing does not satisfy you, have the courage to try something else ... And in any case, there is an opportunity to find like-minded people. That is why so many in their youth tried non-traditional types of sex in order to understand whether they have a penchant for their gender, for example. The first experience often becomes the only one, if not liked, and otherwise the study of one's own sexuality continues. Since we are created this way and this side of our lives needs attention, is it possible to somehow condemn actions that do not harm others, your partner and yourself personally? We have the right to do whatever we want in our personal, uninterrupted life. In theory, no one should have the right to interfere in what happens between adult capable people, but all the same, there are doubts about the legitimacy of their actions, if they are not welcome in society. There is a question about the moral right to do what you want, but for many hundreds of years it was condemned. Find out for what reasons all this was condemned, whether there are objective reasons for the ban.

Logically speaking, even incest cannot harm society, since the only real risk is the damage to the health of your children. The same risk threatens cancer patients, patients with HIV, etc. If, however, the birth of children is excluded altogether, there are no objective reasons to observe the ban on incest. There is only risk society's condemnation. The same applies to homosexual relationships and other relationships that are still prohibited by law in some countries. Assess the risks, evaluate the degree of harm to yourself and others, and decide what consequences you are ready for, given the degree of society's aggression towards non-traditional relationships. Everything else is your own business.

Unconventional situation

My situation is, to put it mildly, unconventional. In many ways. Today I am a successful, professional woman, attractive, with my own apartment (a gift from my parents) and a car (earned). From my youth, I gravitated towards girls, but, being a "Komsomol activist", I wrote it off more like stupidity a la"You never know what comes to mind." I was married - it didn't work out, novels with men also didn't work out (all on my initiative). No, everything is nice, fine, but not that. Until I decided to follow the lead of my inner "dragons". A relationship began with a girl of my age, and then I realized that ... everything ... I found it, came to life, blossomed. On the one hand, the mind screams something like a "nightmare", and in the heart there is such happiness that it is impossible to convey. I don't shout about my relationship, only my closest friends know about it, and I don't intend to. Just no, no, and the mind begins to spoil the picture. I'd be happy to see it from the outside. Thank you.

Kristina, Kazan, 31 years old

Alyona:

It's very dangerous to ask straight people for "how I look" opinions, Christine. And, most importantly, it does not make the slightest sense. This is almost the same as asking an Orthodox Christian how he feels about Kabbalah. These are, in principle, two parallel existing realities, whatever one may say. From the point of view of morality and faith - you yourself know the answer. From the point of view of biology, same-sex relationships exist even in animals, that is, this is not some kind of "know-how" of a reasonable person. However, there is in the animal world and treason, and fratricide. How to relate to all this depends on upbringing and personal beliefs. If you consider same-sex relationships to be normal for you, if they do not harm anyone, what difference does it make what outsiders, people you do not know, think about it? What will it change in your life? I think nothing. And if so, why ask?

Sergey:

Christina, in my opinion, if you feel good in some respects and everything suits your partner, then what difference does it make what gender him is? In modern times, such relationships are not particularly surprising to anyone, and moreover, in certain environments they are even welcomed. So stop fidgeting. We are all different, and everyone needs something different. And therefore, if you have always been more interested in girls than young people, then so be it. In this case, it will be much worse if you rape yourself and portray “natural". However, if you understand with your head that you are doing something wrong, it is quite possible that your orientation is just an internal protest. Then pretty soon you will get tired of communicating with a girl and you will switch back to men. This also happens, and quite often. Therefore, wait a minute to write yourself down as a representative of non-traditional. Life is a complicated thing. There is a lot in it. Including various deviations. However, time will put everything in its place. Until then, enjoy what you have.

My daughter lives with a girl

I do not even know where to start. Thoughts are confused. I am 53 years old. At 25 I gave birth to a daughter Irina. She gave birth without a husband, for herself. I grew it (and these were the “dashing 90s” - who understands!), I put my whole soul into it. At school, she was a quiet, complaisant, completely homely child, she studied well. And then I entered the university, and then it began. Irina met this girl (here I am writing, but my hands are shaking!) And six months later she moved to live with her with the words: “Mom, I love her.” What I just didn’t do to make Ira come to her senses: she stopped giving money and communicating. Ira left the university and went to work - I cried and asked her to change her mind, but she ran into nothing! She called the parents of this creature, and even talked to her herself, demanded that Irina be left alone and not break the life of my child. And we've been at war for 10 years now. Recently, they quarreled again and the daughter said that she was tired, that she wants to live the way she lives, and not "on someone's orders", that I should accept her for who she is. How to return the daughter to a normal life? I am already 53 years old, I want to nurse my grandchildren!

Nadezhda, Petrozavodsk, 53 years old

Alyona:

I almost had time to sympathize with you in this difficult life situation, but the last phrase cooled me. It turns out that all the emotions about the non-traditional orientation of the daughter are connected with the fact that she did not live up to your expectations and did not provide you with leisure “for those who are over 50”? It's all about the lack of purpose in your life personally, right? Because you expected that at this respectable age you would be busy with grandchildren? You know, Nadezhda, the irony of life is that your daughter doesn't owe you anything. The fact that you gave birth to her "for yourself" and endured hardships and hardships, trying to grow a person out of her, does not mean at all that you have rights to her life now. It is a mistake to perceive your daughter, born "for yourself", as a remedy for loneliness and expect grandchildren from her who will brighten up old age. Your daughter could, for example, not want to have children at all, it is also her right. Or maybe she will have them, but later, like many gay women. But this is only her choice, she certainly should not give birth to YOU grandchildren. Her right to decide whether and when to become a mother.

I agree that the homosexual orientation of a daughter (or son) is not at all what parents would like to see. Such "news" will not make any mother happy, here I completely understand you. But... 10 years is enough time to evaluate what is more precious to you: your daughter, the way she is, or your principles. Say, if your daughter were barren, would you blame her for never having your own grandchildren? And if your daughter did not have legs or arms, would you refuse her, believing that she is not like everyone else? I guess not? So why, after so many years, have you been unable to accept the fact that your daughter is not like everyone else, and that she may never have children of her own, but this is not a reason to spend decades feuding with the person closest to you? Whatever they are she is the only native and dearest person for you. And it was with her that you waged war for 10 years, trying to make her be what you need, instead of communicating with her, sharing joys and sorrows, celebrating holidays, giving gifts to each other, the main of which is the joy of communication ...

In my opinion, instead of trying to "bring your daughter back to normal", you should take care to bring your relationship back to life. Your daughter has not changed in 10 years, despite all your “measures”, which means that this choice is conscious and hard-won for her, and not without your help. It's time to face the truth, if necessary, discuss this problem with a psychologist in personal conversations and start changing not your daughter, but your behavior and attitude to what is happening. 10 years is a long enough time to understand that everything you tried to do does not bring results, but only makes both your daughter and you suffer.

Sergey:

In my opinion, the advice here is completely meaningless. The man who has been fighting for so many years imply cannot look at the situation from a different point of view. After all, even the question is formulated not “how can we figure it out, how can we find common ground”, but “how to return our daughter to a normal life” and “I want grandchildren”. That is, "I want" in the first place. In this regard, I would like to ask: what is a normal life? And did the girl see her, whom her mother gave birth to for herself, trying to make a doll from a living person? Maybe I'm wrong, but I think that in order to create a normal family in the future, a child should see an example of such a family in childhood. Even if it's not your own. An example of a family where there are relationships with men, where people kiss, hug, where the gender of each member of this cell of society is clear. If the girl was brought up by a mother who decided to replace everything with herself, who did not communicate with men, since "they are all goats", which for the same reason forbade communication with boys, then why be surprised? Everything worked out right.

So it is hardly worth blaming the daughter for something. She just lives the way she was taught. What to do next? Change. And I think that in the future not to aggravate an already difficult situation, it is worth starting as soon as possible. There are good practicing psychologists in Petrozavodsk, contact them. I'm sure the process won't be easy, but it's worth it. Perhaps, seeing the changes in you, the daughter will simply understand that there is no point in continuing to protest, and everything will fall into place by itself. In any case, you have to start somewhere. And if in 10 years it was not possible to change others, it is worth thinking about the reason and trying to change yourself. She just lives the way she was taught. What to do next? Change. And I think that in the future not to aggravate an already difficult situation, it is worth starting as soon as possible. There are good practicing psychologists in Petrozavodsk, contact them. I'm sure the process won't be easy, but it's worth it. Perhaps, seeing the changes in you, the daughter will simply understand that there is no point in continuing to protest, and everything will fall into place by itself. In any case, you have to start somewhere. And if in 10 years it was not possible to change others, it is worth thinking about the reason and trying to change yourself. She just lives the way she was taught. What to do next? Change. And I think that in the future not to aggravate an already difficult situation, it is worth starting as soon as possible.

There are good practicing psychologists in Petrozavodsk, contact them. I'm sure the process won't be easy, but it's worth it. Perhaps, seeing the changes in you, the daughter will simply understand that there is no point in continuing to protest, and everything will fall into place by itself. In any case, you have to start somewhere. And if in 10 years it was not possible to change others, it is worth thinking about the reason and trying to change yourself. But it's worth it. Perhaps, seeing the changes in you, the daughter will simply understand that there is no point in continuing to protest, and everything will fall into place by itself. In any case, you have to start somewhere. And if in 10 years it was not possible to change others, it is worth thinking about the reason and trying to change yourself. But it's worth it. Perhaps, seeing the changes in you, the daughter will simply understand that there is no point in continuing to protest, and everything will fall into place by itself. In any case, you have to start somewhere. And if in 10 years it was not possible to change others, it is worth thinking about the reason and trying to change yourself.

Chapter 3

Remembering that a man wants to see in a woman at the same time a housewife, a business woman, a mother of her children and a prostitute in her own bed, many girls strive to meet all these requests as much as possible. And not really thinking: for whom are they trying so hard? At first, it's understandable, for a hypothetical future husband, who is still being chosen and "lured" by his outstanding ... qualities. Well, then you need to keep your faithful so that he does not run away. This is how a lot of people think about it.

Based on this, the desire to improve in sex is most often caused precisely by the dream of pleasing a man, so much so that if he does not stay by his side forever, then at least he will remember later until old age with a dreamy smile ... We also have a feeling of rivalry with other representatives of the beautiful half of humanity: I want to be at least something better than everyone else, and who, if not a man, can become an arbiter in this competition? Remembering that a man wants to see a woman as a housewife, business woman, mother of his children and a prostitute in her own bed, many girls strive to meet all these requests as much as possible.

Feminists have their own take on a woman's aspiration to become a sex goddess: how can you please a man and be like a servant to him, providing an orgasm on the highest level? And in a good way, perfection in the art of carnal pleasures is what the woman herself needs. Just as we want to learn how to cook, dance, etc. perfectly, so in the intimate sphere of life there is a need to achieve a certain level of skill. What about the goal? To please your husband, because you love him and in gratitude for all the good things, plus learn to enjoy yourself.

Unlike geishas and hetaeras, who completely focused their art of sex on a man, a free modern woman studies theory and practice for the sake of harmony in relationships, for the sake of knowing her body and understanding how to please husband.

How can you become a goddess of sex? No, for this it is not necessary to practice on many experimental subjects and gain practical knowledge. Firstly, there are books, and secondly, the Internet with articles and videos, where everything is very clearly shown. This is from shareware content on the topic. There are paid video courses on the Web, where a lot of theoretical information is presented and all the same video lessons are provided.

Finally, offline courses for women have been advertised in recent years. In a hidden room, using dildos and other visual aids, a female trainer shows a group of students how to perform oral sex in three dozen different ways, shares tricks like throat singing while swallowing gourd ... that is, MCH. The coach explains what and how to make a man feel ecstasy and give you a Grand Cherokee in gratitude, and attentive listeners giggle and blush. In general, a nice pastime, if it is at the expense of a man who is interested in what you will please him after school.

Another source of knowledge is the husband himself. He certainly knows what he likes. No need for telepathy - just ask. He may not like the interrogation, then ask in an intimate setting and in an intriguing voice. Let him direct your hand, in the end, confess to something that is interesting to him, but seems too immodest. Focus on his sighs and moans, experiment. If you have doubts about his reaction to certain types of petting, you are afraid of his sharply negative reaction (you never know, some people see perversion in some caresses), ask in advance how he feels about this and that. And I hope such conversations do not frighten him, otherwise how can you even discuss your joint intimate life?

Why doesn't my husband want me?

I got married at 26 for love. My husband loves me. Before marriage, they lived together for one year, the sex was stormy. After the wedding, the husband was changed in terms of sex. It became less and less common, and after six years of marriage it disappeared. At the same time, my husband constantly says that he loves me that everything suits him in our marriage, and the problem is not at all in me. To my repeated attempts to understand what is the reason for the lack of sexual relations, he replies that he is very tired, that all thoughts are about work, about how to earn money for the dacha, to provide materially for our family. Many will say it's great. The husband is serious, responsible, all in the care of the family and the house. But it turns out that we live like brother and sister, the relationship is very warm, close, but without intimacy. Recently, I realized that I myself lost desire for my husband. I don't want to destroy my family, I don't want to change too, But I don't feel like I'm married either. Help me to understand. It seems to me that life is passing by, there are a lot of men around me who like me, have never suffered from a lack of male attention, and sometimes it's even funny and insulting: next to a husband whom you don't attract as a woman, and, for example, one acquaintance who openly says that he has long loved and envied my husband that he has such a wife.

Ksenia, Moscow, 33 years old

Alyona:

Xenia, I would not attach much importance to the words of a friend. He can say anything, but in reality he may not have the same sexual temperament as your husband. After all, your spouse was also keenly interested in sex before the wedding. Well, again, it's one thing - to blow into the ears of a married lady with the secret hope of dragging her into bed, trying her and either making her your mistress, or sending her to ignore after the first sex, realizing that in bed she is the same as other. And it is quite another to have serious intentions towards a free woman. The problem is that many men are greedy for married women precisely because they do not need to be married.

A married woman is the most comfortable type of lover who will not complain, for example, that she had to celebrate the New Year alone because her lover was with the family. Well, and so on. In general, do not flatter yourself too much: most of those who look at you with lust will fall off as soon as you decide to get a divorce. And those who remain ... It's not a fact that in a couple of years the story with her husband will not repeat itself.

As for the problems with the lack of sex in your married couple, there is too little information to advise anything. Not only could your husband change, but you yourself. I'm talking about both physical and behavioral changes. Are you still the same as six years ago? Have your behavior and habits changed since marriage? For some reason, some women are sure that after marriage, you can defile in front of your husband in shorts and a bra, in not very attractive home clothes (often these are some shabby robes, old T-shirts and sports tights), in curlers or with a mask of cucumbers on the face . I'm exaggerating, of course, but it's still worth analyzing: have you definitely not changed since you just met and had rough sex between you? Maybe your husband is not turned on by your homely appearance? Actually, why other men crave you, but not the husband? Perhaps, just because they don't see you in everyday life, you offer them your ceremonial appearance, unlike your husband.

Fatigue, preoccupation with financial problems - all this, of course, also plays a role. But are you doing something yourself so that your husband is less worried about this topic? And, finally, do you yourself at least sometimes take the initiative in sex, or do you expect this from your husband, but you yourself are not active? And if it's customary for you in a couple that the initiative comes from your husband, didn't it turn out that you periodically and not very out of place denied him intimacy, after which he gradually stopped "sticking" to you simply because he began to instinctively fear rejections ? Also plays a role. But are you doing something yourself so that your husband is less worried about this topic? And, finally, do you yourself at least sometimes take the initiative in sex, or do you expect this from your husband, but you yourself are not active? And if it's customary for you in a couple that the initiative comes from your husband, didn't it turn out that you periodically and not very out of place denied him intimacy, after which he gradually stopped "sticking" to you simply because he began to instinctively fear rejections ? Also plays a role.

But are you doing something yourself so that your husband is less worried about this topic? And, finally, do you yourself at least sometimes take the initiative in sex, or do you expect this from your husband, but you yourself are not active? And if it's customary for you in a couple that the initiative comes from your husband, didn't it turn out that you periodically and not very out of place denied him intimacy, after which he gradually stopped "sticking" to you simply because he began to instinctively fear rejections ?

In general, there are more questions than answers, of course. But I think that the problem is not only in the husband. If a man does not want his own wife at all, the role of the wife in this certainly was not the last. So, in addition to asking her husband, it would be nice to dig into yourself.

Sergey:

Ksenia, we are all people, and we are all different. Everyone has their own needs, desires, and their own temperament. Including sexy. For example, there are those who need sex every day, those who are quite satisfied with once a month, but there are also those who do not need sex at all. There are not many of them, of course, only about three percent. But they are. And this difference is only in the physiological type, that is, a purely natural difference, laid down from the very beginning. And when people meet with diametrically opposed needs in this regard, this alone is enough to start problems. Especially if there was only passion between people, but neither love nor respect arose. And if we add here the inevitable decrease in attraction due to addiction, age, fatigue, excitement, fears, depression, illnesses, then the picture is completely bleak. Especially if, for example, a man who initially had an average need for sex lives in constant stress and fatigue, and his wife, the owner of high sexual energy, stays at home, visits beauty salons and dine with girlfriends. And the only problem is that her husband does not appreciate her beauty, because he does not have sex with her daily. And he simply cannot live as actively as she does. As a result, constant showdowns, additional stress and an even worse situation with sex. I think in such cases it is better to just leave and not fool each other. That her husband does not appreciate her beauty, because he does not have sex with her daily. And he simply cannot live as actively as she does. As a result, constant showdowns, additional stress and an even worse situation with sex. I think in such cases it is better to just leave and not fool each other. That her husband does not appreciate her beauty, because he does not have sex with her daily. And he simply cannot live as actively as she does. As a result, constant showdowns, additional stress and an even worse situation with sex. I think in such cases it is better to just leave and not fool each other.

If the family seems to have everything except sex, then you still don't notice something else. For example, many women repeat that their husbands have cooled off towards them, but they abruptly interrupt any attempt by their husband to take the initiative in this matter, since this initiative is always at the wrong time. And this behavior appears after the wedding. It's not the place, it’s not the time, then the dress will be wrinkled, then people will see, and only the head it hurts almost permanently. As a result, after a certain number of attempts, the husband stops taking the initiative, because any refusal in this matter causes a certain injury to male pride. After all, it turns out that they do not want him, that he is not a sexually attractive man. As a result, it is easier for a man to catch the flirtatious glance of a woman who is not burdened with problems on the street and quickly regain his sense of his own masculinity in the gateway than to persuade his beloved, constantly present nearby, understanding wife.

I can also report that for a huge number of husbands, sex at the end of a hard day's work, and even almost late at night, very soon becomes unnecessary. Well, here is such a physiology. But in the morning, when you are still in bed and the man has everything that is possible, he is ready for any feats. But at this moment, the wives' teeth are not brushed, their hair is not combed, and in general, how is it possible in the morning? And the man just does not care deeply about this. He wants sex. As a result, he cannot in the evening, you cannot in the morning, and spontaneous reactions are not accepted during the day. Well, who then is to blame for the fact that there is no sex?

In addition, purely physical changes should not be discounted. Alas, very often people simply do not notice how much they have changed over the years. And if once the husband was sexually active with a slender, high-breasted girl, now he sees something completely different in front of him. And, quite possibly, this other one doesn't turn him on like that. No, for someone else, it is quite possible that a rounded butt, thickened hips and chest are only a joy. Especially if it's just for once, try it. But not to her husband. Or even sadder, a man could suddenly realize that he was a homosexual. As funny as it may seem, there are men who suddenly find out that they love men only after several years of marriage with a woman.

Although it still happens that the problem is not that the husband has cooled off, but that the wife does not really want him. Maybe because he got fat, his character changed not for the better, or he was just tired, but she has long been attracted to other men and she does everything she can to bring the situation to a divorce, but not openly, but in such a way as to be "abandoned type". After all, then it becomes possible to blame everything not on your beloved, but on "this dog".

Also, your husband could just find himself another woman. Alas, if you are pretty, everything is in order, you are ready for sex on demand, and your husband does not want you, and for a long time, then he is either impotent or he has another woman.

In this case, in fact, either to the doctor or to the registry office to file for divorce. What exactly is happening in your case, I personally can't say and I think that it's better for you to contact a specialist. But first, just talk seriously with your husband again. If he loves you, he simply cannot but understand the seriousness of the situation. And if he has health problems, he will find the strength to go for treatment. If not, then, unfortunately, your family life with this man is most likely over and it would be better to start preparing for a divorce.

I love you but don't want to?

I have been married for three years. The husband is ten years older. We have a wonderful relationship, we care about each other, love, we are interested together, if we quarrel, then on domestic issues, rarely and not for long. The problem is this: in the last year we have no sexual attraction to each other. Sex is, but mechanical and twice a month. Although the husband says that he wants, and I push him away; I have the same feeling. We sort of have sex because we want sex, not because we want each other. I started thinking about our family life, looking for reasons - I can’t find them. There is tenderness, my husband kisses me all the time, I hug him, we are pleased, I like his smell, voice ... It hurts me to think about parting, he is my dear and beloved. But it can't go on like this for years. How is it that I love, but do not want? I would appreciate that you or the opinions and advice, I really need them.

Marina, Khabarovsk, 35 years old

Alyona:

Marina, relationships with a loved one cannot be frozen at any one stage, they will develop, whether you like it or not. That intensity of passions, those emotions, those desires that were at the beginning of your relationship hey cannot remain at the same level all your life. Inevitably, the emotional background levels off and it seems that the feelings are no longer “the same”. Two, living together, stop "winning" each other, trying to draw attention to themselves, trying again and again to please. They are already together, already living under the same roof and sleeping in the same bed. They don't have to think of anything to be together. They do not need to charm each other to arouse the desire to have sex. As a result, they themselves find themselves in a kind of trap: they do not need to try for the sake of intimacy, for this, it is enough just to lie down in bed (because a spouse will lie next to you) and stretch out your hand. So it turns out that sex is becoming something as commonplace as brushing your teeth. But, of course, to part with a loved one because of this is stupid. Firstly, because with any other partner you are likely to find yourself in exactly the same situation. Secondly, it is not a fact that you will generally find the same native and congenial person as your husband.

In my opinion, everything is fixable if you set out to add romance to your relationship. It may seem artificial at first, but the main thing is to start. When was the last time you were alone in a cafe or restaurant? When did you go to the cinema together? When did you arrange a candlelit dinner for yourself with beautiful music (you don't have to cook it yourself, you can order takeaway food so as not to kill yourself at the stove before you light the candles)? Maybe you should do something together in your free time, something that will unite you, that will emphasize your sexuality for each other? For example, a joint sport? Or pair dancing? There are a lot of options on how to diversify your life with your loved one. I had a couple I knew who, on principle, slept in different rooms, and they were in the same bed only when they really wanted intimacy. So I advise you not to get hung up on the presence of a problem, but to look for options on how to make your couple richer in impressions. Then it will be much easier with the desire to possess each other, and not just sexual discharge.

Sergey:

Marina, someone needs it often and in a variety of ways, someone is almost indifferent to sex. It depends on many reasons. Age, health status, depression, physical inactivity, physical and psychological fatigue, hormonal levels, family relationships, habits and much more. In addition, the sexual behavior of the family develops along with the family.

In youth or at the beginning of a relationship, in most cases, emotions are in full swing, but over time, passion inevitably goes away. I'm sure you yourself understand all this very well. You are old enough to realize that you cannot have sex like unencumbered boys and girls. It's just physically impossible.

So your problem, it seems to me, is not the number of sexual contacts per month. In this regard, any number of intercourses per year is permissible, as long as it suits both spouses. It's about family relationships, which began to change. Maybe the roles have changed. This happens quite often. Especially during periods of some kind of personal crisis. And if at the beginning of a relationship, for example, you were emotionally dependent on your husband, subordinate to him, and he was a dashing eagle on a horse, and now for some reason you have become stronger and more determined, and he is the opposite, then there is nothing strange in that your sex life has also changed. He became afraid of you. And it is quite possible that you do not even understand why. However, sometimes a man needs only one refusal to start feel insecure.

I will give a real example of one pair. They lived for a while, everything was as usual. And then the wife went up the quarry ladder. It is clear that worries appeared, she began to get tired. And at some point my wife was not in the mood. Her head hurt, something else, and she suddenly reacted to his flirting differently than usual. Refused. It seems to be a trifle, but a problem may well grow out of it. Especially if the husband had trouble at work at that moment, he suddenly realized that he was starting to get better, a midlife crisis had attacked or something else. As a result, the old system broke down. He became afraid to make proposals, because he was afraid of being rejected. After all, this is a blow to self-esteem. And the man began to pretend that he did not need it at all. After a while, the wife began to "strain." According to women's tradition, she wound herself up, of course.

Alas, most families face a similar problem. And not everyone manages to solve it. Here, in my opinion, it all depends on the quality of the relationship. If people really love each other, if they know how to talk and solve internal problems, then everything will settle down and normalize over time. If not, then the case may end in disappointment and divorce. So I suggest you start talking frankly with each other. Maybe something happened, maybe there was a misunderstanding or mistrust. We need to clarify the situation, to explain. I'm sure things will get easier later on. So, let's continue to discuss all sorts of ways to savvy in theory and practice thanks to various manuals. Is there any point in all this preparation? Definitely yes.

Firstly, you will learn many interesting options for arranging a holiday out of the marriage night. And for both of you. At least worth a try. And when asked where the new knowledge comes from, nod to the Internet, reassure the man. Or better yet, pretend it's your own fantasy, why not? The main thing is that you feel good.

Start by exploring erotic massage. A very pleasant way to help your husband relax and enjoy the fact that you seized the initiative from him. Remember how men who come to Thailand are eager to experience the Thai massage first thing, which local heterosexuals perform using their own breasts. Why not repeat this at home? A lot of oil, a few tricks peeped on YouTube - and now you are already mentally in an exotic country, on the seashore, enjoying previously unknown sensations.

It is not difficult to learn oral sex from video tutorials, and this is a mandatory quality of a sex goddess, as you understand. If the taste and smell are disgusting, persuade your husband to take a shower together, coat him with chocolate syrup, in the end. Even porn films are very educational, if they do not disgust you. In the field of sex, so many things have been invented over many millennia that it is a sin not to use what you are interested in.

One of the most popular techniques is wimbling. This is a program for the development of female intimate muscles, based on the exercises of the gynecologist A. Kegel. In fact, these secrets have been known to mankind for a very long time. Priestesses of love passed them on to their students from century to century and demonstrated this art by holding various objects with the muscles of the vagina in front of the eyes of the astonished public. The main goal of these exercises was the ability to compress and unclench the muscles of the vagina, narrowing it and clasping the MFC. A man experiences unusual and impressive sensations while a woman squeezes his genitals, as if stroking him from the inside, changing the rhythm and intensity of these "strokes". Spicy addition to regular sex! But that's not all. Thus, the woman herself enjoys, because it increases blood circulation in the muscles, narrowing them,

After childbirth, many ladies have stretched muscles in a secret place, so that for the first months an unpleasant impression is created that the MFC is lost somewhere there, and the sensations become dull. Than a man try to do the almost impossible and increase the thickness of her genitals, it is easier for a woman to do her "physical training" and regain her former shape, especially since intimate plastic surgery in most cases can be replaced by the same wimbling.

Kegel exercises are recommended for:

– for effective preparation for the upcoming pregnancy and successful painless childbirth;

– pregnant women to learn complete relaxation of those muscles that usually prevent the baby from being pushed out during childbirth;

– for the prevention and treatment of urinary and fecal incontinence;

– for recovery after childbirth of tissues that have experienced strong stretching;

– for the prevention and treatment of prolapse of the pelvic organs;

– for long-term maintenance of sexual health,

prevention of inflammatory processes in the genital area, resistance to the effects of aging on the body.

So, as you can see, the goal here is not only the desire to please a man, scolded by feminists, but also the benefit to your health.

The exercises themselves are varied: from simple to complicated by the use of special simulators: vaginal balls, such as “egg”, etc. But you don’t need to be afraid of all this. The main thing is not the number and complexity of exercises, but their consistent application. It takes from a couple of weeks to several months of daily exercises to feel your muscles in intimate places and learn how to control them.

First, it is recommended to feel the muscles that need to be trained. The pelvic floor muscles are responsible for urinary retention. Remember the sensations when you urgently need to stop urination, and you will understand what exactly you need to squeeze and unclench. Gradually, during training, you will find that you can distinguish which muscles are responsible for the anus, which for the area around the clitoris, which for the vagina. But at first it will be difficult, just do the right amount of compressions and do not get disappointed ahead of time.

Exercise 1.

Contract your muscles and relax 30 times in a row. Try doing it at different speeds.

Exercise 2.

Squeeze your muscles and count to 30. Relax.

Exercise 3

Try "pushing out", open up as much as possible, and so on 30 times.

There are many more variations of the technique, look on the Internet. This is enough for a good result, but there is always an opportunity to improve your skills.

How realistic is it to master the technique? Absolutely real. Usually, all these advertising promises are encouraging, but it is difficult to believe in them. However, in this case, three exercises that take 3-5 minutes every day are really enough to feel the result in a month or two and be able to try out a new technique on her husband during sex. It is best to get into the habit of doing Kegel exercises daily and constantly to prevent bladder failure and keep fit, so to speak. Use your free minute to your advantage while standing in line or in any other situation of forced waiting. By the way, keep in mind that outwardly your actions are not visible, but there is evidence that men react quite violently to a woman squeezing her vaginal muscles: they instinctively feel her sexual appeal.

How to explain the lack of desire on his part?

Long story... I'm 37 years old, he's my age. He is

my man, my husband. Married 20 years. Children - a boy and a boy, already adults. A grandson was born last year. I attractive, he's damn attractive. In relation to children, we are often mistaken for brother and sister. Both make good money. Love ... I don’t know what love is, only I feel bad without him. We often joke that since we got married on February 29, we lived only 5 years. I am not a gift. If you evaluate critically, then I am no hostess. I am a creative person, I am fond of sewing, so chaos is my natural habitat. We are like two opposites. Dirty dishes, if they stand evenly and do not violate the overall harmony of the correct lines, do not bother me at all. It irritates him directly physically ... I don’t like cooking at all. In general, he grumbles, and I listen. He is a brutal man, he can say rude things. I translate as a joke or trudge doomed to the kitchen when I feel that conflict is unavoidable. This is about us in general terms. The essence of the problem is as follows. We have different temperaments. I'm talking about sex. If I do not take the initiative, then the "moratorium" on sex can last more than a month. Lingerie does not turn him on, and he is used to my various sexy outfits - I have been sewing since the sixth grade and I am not used to dressing traditionally. I tried to become a home bunny, I even cooked compote - it only yawns and falls asleep. What to do and how to explain the lack of desire on his part?

Olga, Novokuznetsk, 37 years old

Alyona:

Olga, you have been married for 20 years, is it really impossible to ask your husband this intimate question? After all, this is the most natural thing in your situation. For so many years, in theory, you should have already reached the level of relations when such issues can be resolved together. Or are you afraid that the answer to this question will hurt you too deeply? Personally, I do not think that the problem lies in the fact that you are "no hostess." Moreover, attempts to become an exemplary housewife did not justify themselves, as you write. Rather, it is a matter of age, habit, fatigue. Lack of initiative on the part of a husband may mean nothing but a lack of sexual temperament. And for sure this "problem" in your pair has always been. Perhaps, at a younger age, the husband was a little more active, more cheerful, but that's all. In my opinion, there is no need to dig very deep. If, say, we were talking about that a few years ago he was a real stallion, and then he suddenly cooled off, began to come home late and showed little interest in you - yes, there would be something to worry about. But your husband, as I understand it, is a goof on this part for life. To break it or re-educate, perhaps, too late. And the fact that he responds to your initiative is not the worst solution to the problem of your sex life. Well, again, how trusting and close are you really? To what extent are you able to discuss the problems that arise in your couple (in the family)? If possible, then discuss what is troubling you with your husband and, in a playful, joking manner, set a schedule of "duties", create a calendar of marital initiatives together, finally.

There would be something to worry about. But your husband, as I understand it, is a goof on this part for life. To break it or re-educate, perhaps, too late. And the fact that he responds to your initiative is not the worst solution to the problem of your sex life. Well, again, how trusting and close are you really? To what extent are you able to discuss the problems that arise in your couple (in the family)? If possible, then discuss what is troubling you with your husband and, in a playful, joking manner, set a schedule of "duties", create a calendar of marital initiatives together, finally. There would be something to worry about. But your husband, as I understand it, is a goof on this part for life. To break it or re-educate, perhaps, too late. And the fact that he responds to your initiative is not the worst solution to the problem of your sex life. Well, again, how trusting and close are you really? To what extent are you able to discuss the problems that arise in your couple (in the family)? If possible, then discuss what is troubling you with your husband and, in a playful, joking manner, set a schedule of "duties", create a calendar of marital initiatives together, finally.

How trusting and close are you really? To what extent are you able to discuss the problems that arise in your couple (in the family)? If possible, then discuss what is troubling you with your husband and, in a playful, joking manner, set a schedule of "duties", create a calendar of marital initiatives together, finally. How trusting and close are you really? To what extent are you able to discuss the problems that arise in your couple (in the family)? If possible, then discuss what is troubling you with your husband and, in a playful, joking manner, set a schedule of "duties", create a calendar of marital initiatives together, finally.

Sergey:

As far as I know men, none of them can burn with eternal, constant sexual passion for the same woman. It's physically impossible. After all, no matter how a goat a man rides in his youth, no matter what storms of passion rage between partners, time inevitably extinguishes the colors. Then the house, children, worries, life, and age one way or another take their toll. In addition, over the years, responsibility often increases, and hence the burden. A person begins to get tired much cornier, and at the same time, the recovery time does not even think to decrease. Quite the opposite. Stress is again ubiquitous, fears growing over the years. Therefore, there is nothing strange in the fact that after 20 years of marriage, your husband does not want to have sex every day. We are not getting younger, and therefore even those who jumped on everything that moves, in their youth, by middle age they lose such a stormy interest in this process. Especially if there was nothing at the heart of the family except for naked teenage passion.

No, of course, with the appearance of a young, new lover, interest is renewed for a while. But not for long. As far as I know, in order for the spouses to keep their interest in each other, it is necessary that there was something real, big and bright between them from the very beginning. You, as I understand it, had nothing of the kind. Therefore, if you dream of the renewal of passion, then these are completely vain hopes. And if you are mainly concerned about this, then as an option you can have a young hot lover. Another option is to just talk frankly with your husband and dot the "Yo". After all, after all, your children are already adults, but you yourself are still relatively young. So why waste time on something that neither you nor your husband need anymore? In such conditions, rather than spoil each other's nerves, it is better to remain good friends and start looking for something new.

Well, we are all talking about techniques, methods of sex, and the secrets of the goddess of sex are not only high-class petting and body work. It is also psychological techniques, and appearance. After all, sex is not a separate, unrelated area of our life, it affects family life and well-being, and many extraneous factors affect the quality of intimacy.

What affects the quality of sex?

Situation

If someone can suddenly interfere, if you can't scream for your own pleasure, if it's uncomfortable and diapers are lying around or simply untidy, this can cool desire and reduce pleasure. True, it is worth noting that the risk of exposure sometimes, on the contrary, excites beyond measure. And it is certainly extremely pleasant to have sex, if not with a new partner, then in a new environment, on vacation, in a new city, country, by the sea, in a car, etc., etc.

Mood

It's good to unwind by making love to your husband (wife), and forget about troubles and resentments that are not related to your partner. But when the level of emotions goes off scale, it can be difficult to distract yourself, and sex may even become impossible for this time. And if a quarrel with a spouse is to blame, then anorgasmia and other troubles may generally occur, and there will be no excitement, only resentment and grief. So try not to quarrel and quickly put up, sort things out more delicately, without threats and insults, and even more so with violent methods. Do not put off reconciliation for later, it cools the relationship more than a quarrel. How does it say? Better a good quarrel than a bad peace? So follow this rule. Otherwise, you will get used to pouting at each other and mutual affection, which has become a habit, will cease to be an indispensable condition for your family to exist.

Do not put off reconciliation for later, it cools the relationship more than a quarrel. Never, NEVER take your problems and quarrels to bed. All these thoughts and - even worse - conversations, firstly, cause cooling, because it is not possible to relax and be distracted. And secondly, how will your bed then differ from everything else around, will it then be a secluded love nest, intended only for pleasure, with which the only associations are memories of delicious minutes and hours together?

Never, NEVER take your problems and quarrels to bed.

The only option when a quarrel is combined with a bed is a stormy reconciliation, when a high-profile scandal is resolved by hurricane sex, where the ancient powerful instinct, the passion for violence, is quenched in an easy and pleasant way. Not a bad way, by the way, to bring brightness to relationship and defuse tension. Check if this is why you quarreled again?

But a good day, a great mood cause an upliftment of the soul and not only, so take advantage of these moments, celebrate good luck together!

Appearance of partners

This question is, of course, a tricky one. First, lovers maintain an ideal appearance in front of each other, try to preen themselves both in the morning and at night, before meeting with a partner in bed. After getting married or just starting to live together, many stop trying so hard, since it seems like they are already connected together and you don't have to care so much about creating a good impression. Someone still holds on for several years, but breaks down during maternity leave, because fatigue, lactation, stretch marks and depression, and you don't need to go to work, which disciplined you before. In general, we understand intellectually that houses should also maintain a decent appearance. But after all, we see each other in any, as they say, forms, in illness and weakness, in all unsightly situations. The romantic image is crippled, the mood is not always there, so that at home, in native walls,

There is also such that some men can hardly endure the unkempt appearance of their wife, while others love her with all her shortcomings. But even for yourself, it's better to look good, if not great, every day. Some men generally like to possess the woman they like before she takes a shower, with all her natural scents, but this is a matter of individual preference. After all, someone likes to touch the clean skin of a partner, so do not deprive each other of such joy.

Changes in appearance can happen not through our fault, but due to illness, pregnancy, childbirth or breastfeeding, or maybe because of banal laziness. In any case, you should try to adjust your appearance - not only for the sake of attracting the attention of your husband, but also for a pleasant feeling of your own beauty, to regain confidence in your own attractiveness. Although there are happy women whom men admire even with radical changes in their appearance, since men are interested in the woman herself, and her appearance is not a matter of primary importance. But is it worth checking all this for yourself?

The appearance of a woman has played a big role at all times. Chinese noble ladies have been subjected to the horrifying procedure of foot binding since childhood. Their legs were deformed in such a way that they could no longer walk normally. But their duck-like walk, slow, with swaying hips, was considered extremely sexy. One can recall other examples of women mutilating themselves according to the canons of their era in order to be recognized as beautiful and taken as wives. Now we are trying to attract the attention of men with makeup, outfits and other attributes, slimness and a magnificent bust are in fashion, but, fortunately, different men admire different types of women, so short stature can be your advantage, and a magnificent figure, and a hooked nose - there will always be someone to whom exactly your external data will seem to be your advantage, not a disadvantage. You need to try to adjust your appearance - not only for the sake of attracting the attention of your husband, but also for a pleasant feeling of your own beauty, to regain confidence in your own attractiveness.

Attitude towards sex

There is also such a nuance: how do you feel about intimacy and what does your husband think about him. Whole volumes can be written about this, describing each option - from the ironic attitude to the bashful, from the cynical to the indifferent. Each couple develops their own rituals: who starts first, what is possible and what is undesirable, the rules of protection, etc. Insist whether you are in sex, who is the leader, who is the follower, will you endure something for the sake of your partner's pleasure or will you refuse, dodge it or is glad for every touch ... All these family subtleties are revealed and formed gradually during a life together and affect how everything is in an intimate way. The goddess of sex does not evade him and gets as much pleasure from him as a man (or maybe more), she feels the mood of a man and, in accordance with it, takes the initiative or humility, passion or tenderness, fawns or lets out her claws like a cat . And he also shows imagination, surprises and delights with his magnificent, royal appearance and behavior. Difficult? Quite affordable, in my opinion.

State of health

Sometimes a bad mood is a sign of an incipient disease, and if there are already specific health problems, there is no time for sex. Especially if the troubles are connected with the genitals. Any discomfort must be cured by contacting doctors, otherwise intimate life will not cause the most pleasant sensations.

Artificial pathogens

To cheer up, kindle passion, you can use some proven means. Various foods and drinks are used as aphrodisiacs, but not all of them work unambiguously.

For example, alcohol excites someone, while someone completely excludes sex due to the physiological characteristics of the body. But it is definitely worth trying all the recipes that do not harm the body.

Whether to become a hippopotamus again to please her husband?

I no longer like my husband. The fact is that I lost 15 kg. Now I really like myself, and everyone I know tells me that I began to look better. One husband does not like my figure. As he says, "only bones, and nothing to hold onto." And this despite the fact that when we met, I was as thin as I am now, I recovered already when we had been together for a long time, on a hormonal background. Now my hips and chest have really lost a lot of weight - such a physique that all the fat accumulates mainly on the stomach. That is, if I want to get better again, I will get better, with my tendency to be overweight, this is not difficult. But then my huge belly will grow again, and only then everything else ... I don’t want to become a hippopotamus again. But the husband says that it is better to be fat, but with a big booty and breasts. How to be? Should I become a hippopotamus again to please my husband and to the detriment of my self-esteem? Or do you like yourself and others, but with a high probability of losing your beloved man (or enduring his betrayals with "donuts")?

Yana, Perm, 21 years old

Alyona:

Yana, the plan of action is as follows. First: to reassess values and understand that if for a man the main thing in a woman is boobs and buttocks, then you need not to eat your ass, criticized for its skinny appearance, but to grab it and take it away from such a highly intelligent stallion. Second: stop telling yourself the idea that a man has the right to cheat on his wife if she is not Pamela Anderson or Jessica Simpson. If the husband went left because of the body subtraction of his wife, subtract the husband from your life, no one needs such a husband for nothing. What happens when you start to wrinkle? To endure the betrayals of the "beloved" with young girls, justifying them with their external imperfection due to not the first freshness? Or, if he starts criticizing your lips, will you run to a plastic surgeon for silicone ones? This is crazy, Yana.

At 21, you must first of all like yourself. And there will definitely be someone who likes you the way you are. Talking seriously about "holding on to a woman's boobs" - the level of degenerates and cattle. It's better not to mess with such people in life at all, but since it happened, run away from this while you are young. And never change something in your own appearance for the sake of someone's taste and desire. Look at Jocelyn Wildenstein (if you don't know who it is, ask Yandex) and understand that sacrificing your appearance in order to please a man is the path to self-destruction.

And if someone tries to impose on you the idea that you are imperfect, this is your enemy. It's a pity that your official husband became it (or are you not yet scheduled?). But the good news is that you are only 21 years old and it will not be difficult to change it for another. Everything is simple here: if you don't like it, don't eat it, and if you eat it, then shut up.

Sergey:

Yana, in my opinion, you should first consult a doctor. I don't know what you mean by "for a long time", but judging by the fact that you are only 21 years old, and you hardly got married at 17, it turns out that in just a couple of years your weight has changed very seriously twice. At the same time, as I understand it, you did not become pregnant, did not bear, and did not give birth. No, of course, this may be due to age-related changes, but I would still check. The fact is that a sharp change in body weight may well be associated, for example, with developing diabetes. And in this case, it is better to recognize the enemy in advance in person, since in the early stages it is quite possible to agree with this disease in a good way. As for the husband's behavior, I think he needs to be given time to get used to. Hope, his statements are just the fruit of a bad upbringing, or an attempt in this way to justify problems with his own figure. This also happens quite often. If so, then everything will pass by itself after a while.

It would also be nice to talk to him frankly and explain the reason why you do not want to get fat again. I am sure that if you have a normal relationship, then he will understand everything and will even be proud. Or, if this is normal for you and you agree, there is always the possibility of plastic surgery for breast augmentation. But this is only if you yourself agree. If your faithful only married "boobs" and neither agrees nor understands anything, then all the more you should not follow the lead and turn into a hippopotamus again. In this case, alas, nothing good shines for you in any way. After all, we all, alas, do not get younger with age. In addition, a woman's breasts tend to change quite dramatically before, during and after pregnancy. And that will be, if your breasts collapse after feeding? Will your husband leave you alone with your child? So is it worth it to continue this relationship?

Chapter 4

Everything that you can try in sex with your husband and that does not cause you unequivocal rejection is worth trying to give newness to the relationship. It is clear that absolutely everything should not be included in practice from the first days, so that there is something to have fun in the future.

The boundaries of sex can be expanded without fear that these exotic techniques need to be repeated every day. That is the charm of the exotic, that it is interesting only because of its inaccessibility. However, if you both like bed games with a vibrator - great, use it for your pleasure. In sex shops, it is now available and very colorfully talk about the purpose of all devices for diversity in sex. Imitations of the genitals from different materials, different sizes, different degrees of plausibility, mechanical devices with vibration, double and triple vibrators, handcuffs, fancy dress, lubricants, etc., etc. Many couples do not accept sex toys, but you should not immediately discard this idea, at least leave it until difficult times.

Here is what Cleo readers write:

I think no man wants to compete with a rubber toy from shop (but there are those who are turned on by it), their self-esteem decreases from the fact that they were exchanged for cold, "insensitive". Maybe if we are a little kinder to them, we will get everything in abundance and there will be no need for any dildos, although ... sometimes a toy is better ... =)

Asya

Once upon a time, my future husband and I went to such a store ... and even bought something, tried it - laughed) It lay around for a long time, then they threw it away. In short, I am for harmony without nozzles-additives-add-ons-vibrators, although I cannot call myself a conservative in this regard.

Hope, Moscow

Here you live with your husband for 25 years, go again and buy, and you won't throw it away :-)

Elena, Ukraine

But in addition to all this diversity, I would like to mention special ways to expand the scope of what is permitted in sex, which do not require a visit to a sex shop. Particular intimacy is associated, for example, with joint washing in the shower or bath. Covering each other in lather, using water jets in an unconventional way, letting a man shave his bikini area... We'll talk about the kitchen later, but think about the potential of sweet sauces and whipped cream, crushed ice and or hot melted chocolate. Special piquancy, as you know, exists in where you are caught by the desire to make love. It's nice to play tricks on the fresh sheets of the marital bed, but there are even more tempting places for this: the table, the floor, in general, all accessible surfaces in the apartment, and outside it - any secluded corner where you can be caught at the scene of the "crime". In the era of cell phones with a built-in camera, there are more and more videos of such extreme lovers, but many more of those who managed to go unnoticed. Taking risks raises the level of adrenaline in the blood, increases excitement, and memories of the adventure last a lifetime. On a plane, toilet, car, park - wherever it happens! And extreme sex in a tent, forest, on a high mountain? Is it possible to miss this opportunity to have fun and get a unique experience?

Another popular option for developing the topic of sex is to make a porn film about your intimate life. Set the camera aside and throw yourself into each other's arms. And then consider in detail how you look from the outside. And you can also call the operator to enhance the extremeness. Just make sure that it doesn't work out like some Hollywood actresses: their lovers managed to sell home videos with celebrities for a lot of money, glorifying them all over the world.

A less exotic option is to put a mirror nearby and observe the process from two angles at the same time. And for someone, such an action as masturbation in front of a partner is unusual and fascinating.

Men, by the way, are generally big fans of peeping, so use it to your advantage: try cleaning in a light dressing gown on a naked body or in fishnet underwear, let a man open up unexpected angles while you bend down to the bottom shelf ... It turns on many people very quickly !

Role-playing games are a great way to wake up a volcano of passions, if we discard false modesty. You can start with something simpler: a teacher, a little girl with pigtails, etc., and then you can connect costumes and attributes. Some couples reacquaint themselves weekly, meeting in cafes and pretending they are different people. Play Sleeping Beauty, try not to react to petting and keep a serious face, this also turns on many couples.

There are also special ways to add spice to relationships that are not so easy allow: for example, fisting or "golden shower". It is your right to decide on such an extreme, or to refuse, and not all men think about this and accept it. Each of us has our own limits of what is permitted, and it is useless to cross them in order to save the relationship, because this alone will not help save the marriage, and your or his discomfort will not give your relationship an atmosphere of trust.

The main thing in gaining new experience is not to force and not be negative about the partner's initiative, then you will be really pleased and interested together.

I don't want to have sex with my husband

I have a problem with my husband. I don't want to have sex with him at all. We've been married for five years. Lately, sex has been like a duty. And the thing is, it's always the same thing. He never starts anything and is used to having a woman hung around his neck already ready. I do not feel desired at all, since I constantly need to convince him that I want him to the point of impossibility. We talked about this a million times, he says that he cannot do otherwise, but sex is very important to him. We have already tried different toys, then I got tired of it all, I absolutely don't want to start anything, it's even disgusting to think. The last time he said that I was the most boring in this regard and completely unable to interest. We have a wonderful relationship in everything else, we spend almost all our free time together. I don't want to get divorced because of sex, but I see no other way. He hasn't spoken to me for the past five days and thinks it's my fault. The only thing holding me back is my papers, this year we are being tested and we need to be married with proof.

Anna, New York, USA, 30 years old

Alyona:

Is everything so good in everything else, if everything is so bad in sex? Maybe your joint pastime is because you don't have so many other opportunities for leisure so far? Another country, a narrow social circle, a cultural and language barrier (one way or another) - that's the whole secret of the fact that you still hold on to each other. And, of course, the same "check" that you write about. I believe that the countdown to your marriage has already been started for a long time and it's only a matter of time. Your husband's behavior in sex is just a litmus test of your relationship. Your husband blames problems in sex on you, you - on him. But in fact, the problem is something else: you are not interested in each other as sexual partners. In order for your husband to want you, you need to convince him, in fact, beg for sex, imitating a passion that does not exist. You don't need sex with him at all. Was it different before? Or were you just more willing to play the forced role before? In my opinion, you had problems before, but you needed each other (moving, citizenship, etc.), so you turned a blind eye to many things. And now patience is almost exhausted.

I don't think you should force yourself to have sex with your husband if you don't need it and it's disgusting. At a minimum, this is some kind of strange and useless violence against oneself. You are only 30 years old, can't you find a man whom you will really desire physically and who will want you without dancing at the pole? If you really need to "pass the test" - well, hold on to it, and after that quickly stop wasting each other's time. But you needed each other (moving, citizenship, etc.), so you turned a blind eye to many things. And now patience is almost exhausted. I don't think you should force yourself to have sex with your husband if you don't need it and it's disgusting. At a minimum, this is some kind of strange and useless violence against oneself. You are only 30 years old, can't you find a man whom you will really desire physically and who will want you without dancing at the pole? If you really need to "pass the test" - well, hold on to it, and after that quickly stop wasting each other's time.

But you needed each other (moving, citizenship, etc.), so you turned a blind eye to many things. And now patience is almost exhausted. I don't think you should force yourself to have sex with your husband if you don't need it and it's disgusting. At a minimum, this is some kind of strange and useless violence against oneself. You are only 30 years old, can't you find a man whom you will really desire physically and who will want you without dancing at the pole? If you really need to "pass the test" - well, hold on to it, and after that quickly stop wasting each other's time. Can't you find a man whom you will really desire physically and who will want you without dancing at the pole? If you really need to "pass the test" - well, hold on to it, and after that quickly stop wasting each other's time. Can't you find a man whom you will really desire physically and who will want you without dancing at the pole? If you really need to "pass the test" - well, hold on to it, and after that quickly stop wasting each other's time.

Sergey:

In my opinion, if you cannot find mutual understanding on some issue, then the rest is the same. Therefore, your phrase about the fact that everything else wonderful, nothing more than fiction. Your husband does not want to change, does not want to meet you halfway, and is not going to compromise, providing a simple choice: either in my opinion, or not at all. It is unlikely that a person who behaves in such an important matter in such a way is white and fluffy in another. This is your intra-family style of behavior, your rules that you suddenly no longer like. It's just that for the rest it's easier for you to put up with something or not notice something. In this regard, I would venture to suggest that your relationship has come to another crisis, and how it will end, I will not undertake to guess.

Unfortunately, no one knows how to get out of such situations calmly and without losses. There is a huge amount of scientific work on this subject, even more theories, and practicing family therapists who make money in this field, especially in the United States, simply cannot be counted. And yet, people still come to a standstill and divorce in depressing numbers. Therefore, there are no rules of conduct that guarantee success in this situation. Yes, success is different for everyone. Judging by the letter, you yourself do not burn with passion for your husband and would have left long ago, but you hold a purely practical interest. In addition, you don't even stutter about children, and your husband, apparently, also does not burn with the desire to become a father. That is, there is no question of saving the family. The question, rather, stands like this: how to survive a year so that the husband does not send, because you need to pass a test? If so, then probably just be patient and take your time. Suggest to the husband, for example, to address to the family psychotherapist. It will take a couple of months for sure. Then you can say sick or very busy, and for a whole month you can safely do without hateful sex. Then come up with something else. The main thing is to stand for a year and hold out for a day. Well, then you will honestly tell your husband that he is the most uninteresting lover in your life, and you will leave with your head held high.

I want to give him a trip to the strip club

I am 21 years old, and I have been dating a young man, my age, for 1 year and 8 months. Our relationship is very warm and emotional, but I feel that he lacks variety in bed, new experiences. The fact is that I am his first girlfriend in every sense of the word. I know that he is fond of watching adult films, he watches them alone, and sometimes he also buys various toys in sex shops for self-satisfaction. Several times during conversations "heart to heart," he confessed to me that he dreams of being surrounded by many girls, making love to the three of us, even offered to order a call girl. I am very jealous of him, but at the same time I understand that if I want to keep him, I must give him freedom, otherwise he may soon think about "adventures" on the side. In two weeks it will be his birthday, and I seriously thought about choosing a gift. I want to give him an unforgettable experience. I came up with a bold idea - a joint visit to a strip club. The idea is interesting in itself and excites even my imagination, I have already thought of everything, and even the place has already been chosen, but ... doubts do not leave me! Firstly, I don't know what his reaction will be, and secondly, I'm afraid for myself: what if I can't restrain myself, hide my jealousy, I'll break out on him and the holiday will be ruined? Thirdly, I'm just afraid for the further development of our relations... Tell me, what is the right thing to do? I would not want to consult with him, so as not to spoil the surprise. I'm afraid to make a mistake...

Ekaterina, Moscow, 21 years old

Alyona:

Well, firstly, only a completely inexperienced girl in matters of sex can say that the thought of visiting a strip club excites her imagination. Such a statement makes me think that everything is very simple and clumsy in bed with you and your boy. And on both sides, not just yours. Hence the erotic fantasies your boyfriend. I wouldn't be surprised if self-satisfaction with toys from a sex shop is all that he is capable of on his own in a sexual relationship. This, alas, and the group sex will not help.

Why does he not offer you to diversify your relationship? Why, instead of engaging in the exciting process of developing his own sexuality and that of his partner, does he masturbate in front of the TV? Perhaps because in sex he wants to play a passive role, the role of a man being pleased and satisfied, and not the active role of a hero-lover? Otherwise, why indulge yourself with silicone and porn pictures when there is a coveted living woman nearby - an unplowed field for sexual experiments and exploits? Why not buy sensible books on sex techniques instead of toys and porn CDs? Books that would help you understand how to achieve sexual diversity in a couple, and not with the help of experienced prostitutes, strippers or gangbang?

All in all, I don't think you need to drag your boyfriend to a strip club. It's better to buy beautiful sexy lingerie for yourself with this money, and for him a good, colorful, with pictures and photographs manual on sex in a couple and offer to organize a joint reading and study of it step by step. And if he refuses, run away from him. If a man does not think about his partner being good in sex, he will be the same uncouth selfish user in other areas. And fidelity is not to be expected from this.

Sergey:

I would not advise getting carried away with permissiveness just so that the guy does not run away to the side. After all, they are essentially the same thing. And why did you suddenly decide that you should fight for a young man, spread out before him? Why do you? Don't mutual feelings imply mutual responsibility? Or is it that your feelings are not mutual and it is you who are trying to earn the favor of a young man? If so, then earning a guy's love by arranging trips to a striptease is a losing idea.

Although, to be honest, in this particular case, any undertaking is a losing one. I saw a lot of boys and girls. I saw who and how built pairs. So, the more freedom in a relationship, the less time it takes for young people to break up. And I can tell you in all honesty that a man who tells his girlfriend that he wants to have a threesome, foursome or whatever, doesn't love that girl. He just plays, learns, has fun, and satisfies lust. And you're just one of those who help him in this. No more. Nothing serious will come of your relationship.

And I want to say something for the future. You're a woman. You are the mother of future children. And the more responsible, sincerely loving and subtle person will be there, the better. Your current boyfriend is unlikely to meet at least one of these criteria. So next time, try to choose a normal man as your partner, not a horny teenager. As for a birthday present, why don't you invite the young man to watch scenes from his favorite porn movies starring you? Invite him to invite a couple of friends, and in front of his eyes you will give yourself to them in any poses and options. And he will look. Does he love the exotic? This would be a gift so a gift! I hope he will gladly agree to such an offer and you will send him away.

Chapter 5

A woman came to Confucius and asked how polygamy differed from polyandry.

Confucius placed five teapots and five cups in front of her and said:

– Lei tea in five cups from one teapot. Like?

– Like it, the woman agreed.

– And now vice versa, pour into one cup of five teapots.

Like?

– I like it even more," the woman admitted.

– Stupid! Yelled Confucius. - I ruined such a parable!

This request overtakes some of the women after a dozen years of legal marriage, someone happens to hear it for the first time during the first weeks of passion - the pores of frankness and burning confessions. This idea does not find a response in women in most cases, but the man returns and returns to this issue if he has any hope of persuading her to this sex experiment.

How do women usually respond to an offer to take another "girlfriend" into bed, and how do most people think - a rival?

Absolute "no"

They are horrified, they say that this is unacceptable under any sauce. Sometimes they really think so. And if there are religious prohibitions, strong social attitudes to prohibit such ways to diversify your sex life, you need to say so to your partner. Do not just blame the man for this desire and talk about him with excessive disgust. No, no, it was a simple suggestion, not an order. In order not to scare your partner, not to make him afraid to offer you something in the future (and not only in the field of intimate life, but in general some ways to diversify your life together), try to refuse calmly. Explain why you can't and don't want to. And offer an alternative: role-playing games in bed, etc. Perhaps you should promise to think about this offer for a while - a year or two.

You have the right to refuse, because sex should be mutual and voluntary. To participate in threesome sex only with the body, being disgusted, is an insult to dignity, one's own and partners, who, nevertheless, ideally want not only to enjoy, but also to deliver it. However, this is ideal. Sometimes the initiator is a man who is just realizing his erotic fantasy, and what the rest of the participants in the process experience there is not important to him. Something like watching a porn movie, but in close proximity and even with personal participation. If only his own pleasure is important to him, it is worth recommending that he turn to the help of prostitutes, in the end, this is more honest with respect to everyone. By the way, if your relationship involves long-term, and you don't want to allow yourself such experiments, perhaps an option could be a way out, when a husband realizes his fantasies on the side, and with you he lives an ordinary sex life and shares life. If he really needs it, he will still find an option on how to experience the fantasies that excite his imagination. If he is faithful to you, but he still has such a fantasy and has not yet been realized, how did it happen that you so different - still together? However, in life, when we are afraid of many of our desires, while others do not even realize for many years, this does not happen.

You have the right to refuse, because sex should be mutual and voluntary. To participate in threesome sex only with the body, being disgusted, is an insult to dignity, one's own and partners, who, nevertheless, ideally want not only to enjoy, but also to deliver it.

Why do men have such an idea - a threesome? Firstly, the desire to diversify sensations, to increase the number of organs and body parts involved in such sex. Two women caress at the same time - this seems to be a double pleasure. Secondly, the pride of a male who got two women in his bed at once is a consequence of ancient instincts, when the number of women was a sign and a consequence of the male's priority in the pack due to his physical and intellectual benefits. Therefore, there is a desire to experience this at least once in a lifetime - and then you can tell your friends about how well done he was and immediately persuaded two girls. If not to tell, then at least to know about it and remember. But, of course, at least on the forum, at least anonymously, he will tell how cool he spent that unforgettable night, because he knows: just as he used to envy the storytellers, so now someone will envy him. Threesome sex, when there is only one woman and two men, is exotic, another experience of sensual pleasures, an area of new experiments, therefore, some representatives of the strong half of humanity are ready to do this.

Finally, a man can imagine two beautiful women who take the initiative in their own hands and allow him to relieve himself of the responsibility for giving them pleasure, since they will give it to themselves with each other, not forgetting to please the man. And this is a variant of the dream of passive-contemplative sex - pleasure for the sake of pleasure, without a sense of duty to a partner. By the way, if you ask men, most admit that they enjoy the contemplation of two girls kissing, but they absolutely do not accept two men in the same role. Homophobia is strong among men, but it refers mainly to members of the same sex and much less often affects "pink" couples. Therefore, and also because in the MZHM trio you have to compete with another male for the attention of a single woman, rivalry and jealousy appear, men most often dream of sex with two girls.

Evasive refusal

A woman knows how to get by with hints and omissions, so there are a lot of ways to avoid an unpleasant idea not directly, but hidden. It would seem, say "no" - and that's it. But there is a fear that a man will be disappointed in you, be dissatisfied, leave or secretly go looking for a forbidden fruit to another - "less notorious" (I put in quotation marks, because the question "Who is better: a person open to such experiments or not wanting to go for them? "is unethical, and to figure out whether it is good or bad to love peaches is also stupid, you have the right not to like them and not to try). There is another hope - that a man will return to this topic a couple of times, and then forget, get used to you during this time and not risk destroying relations with you for the sake of some exotic pastime. You never know - he will change his mind.

Therefore, the tactic here is that the woman is playing for time: she offers to try sex with two men first, so that everything is "fair", if she is sure that the jealous husband will definitely not go for it in any case, but this offer will discourage him and it will even become a way to blackmail or tease, making the topic of discussion nothing more than a joke, and not a serious reason for reflection. To laugh it off is generally an elegant way out. You can offer to first establish relationships and learn how to trust each other, in order to then accept someone else into the intimate sphere of life, and this, as you know, takes at least a year, and preferably more. Another way to play for time is to offer to find a girl that both of you will like, and, of course, do not agree with the choice of a husband in any case. By the way, for many men, conversations do not go beyond the proposal, precisely because it is necessary to take active steps, look for and persuade any girl to play the role of the third. Not everyone can handle such active actions and such diplomacy, someone is quite shy, and someone just hopes that it is the wife who will find a candidate for the experiment among her friends.

Agreement

What can make a woman agree to a threesome? In general, there are many reasons. For example, curiosity. Not only men want to experience something new and unknown, women are also interested in extreme sports. Moreover, in her imagination there is already a picture of how two will immediately caress her, and if it is two men, then you can try such options and poses that are otherwise inaccessible, and this is many times increased pleasure. Again, I want to keep a man nearby, or at least just bring him joy. Finally, let's not discount the fact that some girls are drawn to people of the same sex, and then a great opportunity is turned up to try something that has not yet been possible, or to repeat an exciting experience.

Moreover, agreeing to a threesome if you are not interested in intimacy with a third person is probably pointless: it will simply be unpleasant for you to share your emotions with a stranger and uninteresting person, to reveal the secrets of your sexuality to him. It probably won't make you happy. Still, such entertainment is more likely for bisexuals.

Love for three is love?

I don't know how to be. I've been dating a guy for almost a year. It seemed to me that he had feelings for me no less than I felt for him. His only drawback is morbid jealousy. I will not describe what it is ... I think everyone understands. But then, on the eve of my birthday, something strange happened to me ... He invited me to a romantic evening together. Everything was perfect: candles, music, and romance. But soon his best friend came. My boyfriend started insisting on a threesome. Reproaches began that I did not value his opinion, I was embarrassed by it, etc. Perhaps the effect of the situation had an effect, but I agreed. The next morning my friend left and we were alone. I tried to discuss what happened, but was refused. A couple of days later, the situation repeated itself, but this time I categorically refused. Everything seems to be fine, but my boyfriend's jealousy has become unpredictable! Tantrums, quarrels, etc. He begs me not to leave him, although there was no question of this, he says that he is jealous of everyone because he loves me very much. HOW can he love me after this and even more jealous? Or is it considered crazy male love?

Anastasia, Atyrau, Kazakhstan, 26 years old

Alyona:

No, he doesn't love you. You are his property. And the attitude towards you as property: to whom I want - I give it to use, to whom I don't want - I don't give it. Hence such a perverse jealousy - only for those who can potentially take possession of you without his permission. Your boyfriend, for an hour, didn't look at all sorts of "9.5 weeks" and similar "masterpieces" in childhood? Banal and disgusting. It's not at all clear how, after everything that happens to you at the initiative of the "boyfriend", you are still with him. The question of finding yourself a man who would treat you like a woman, and not a doll for sexual experiments, did not arise? But in vain. Further it will only get worse. With age, vices and mental disorders only increase. And judging by your letter, the guy with the head is in trouble.

Sergey:

I think the only thing worth doing in this situation is to run away from the young man as quickly as possible. You will not get anything good from communicating with him. The fact is that, in my opinion, not a single man who is normal in terms of his head will offer his own girlfriend to a friend. And if we add to this his morbid jealousy, obvious hysteria and a tendency to aggression (thank God, so far only verbal), then all the more we can safely raise the question of mental health. Well, what, pray tell, do you expect from a relationship with an inadequate person? Do you want to get hit on the head with something heavy in a fit of jealousy? I think you should stay away from such people. After all, who knows what will come to his mind next time? Yesterday he separated you from a friend, and tomorrow he will want some freak to rape and strangle you in front of his eyes. Do you need it? Would you go away from him before it's too late and while health allows move around on your own.

Husband obsessed with a threesome

My boyfriend is 32 years old, we generally have a frank, open relationship, and the sex is the same: more of everything, hotter. Although outwardly we lead a quiet family life. In general, somehow we casually started a conversation on the topic "It would be nice to see how others have, and we are nearby, but we have love ...", etc., etc. Conclusion: we want to see sex of others, but do not touch us with your hands. A year has passed. We drove, we forgot, and there is no real reason. And in Prague, during dinner, he asks me to go to a brothel, because he really wants to see me with another girl (I told him about my youthful homosexual experience). It will be a complete lie if I write that I went to the brothel with my head bowed. No, I ran with him, it was interesting and tempting. We agreed that she and I do everything, he just watches. This went on for two minutes. Then it turned into a banal "threesome". Then there was another night. Now we are at home. He launched an unrealistic campaign to find a third to us in bed. I'm jealous. He is in seventh heaven with happiness: "You are the MOST close, this is OUR experience, this is what WE shared, and without you I don't need it for nothing (I believe this is a very important moment!!!), you are the best in the world." And even began to call to marry (?). How to stop all this? Or is there really no chance? I really don't want to go from "my adored heathen" to How to stop all this? Or is there really no chance? I really don't want to go from "my adored heathen" to How to stop all this? Or is there really no chance? I really don't want to go from "my adored heathen" to "narrow-minded petty bourgeois". I'm confused.

Natalia, Odessa, 28 years old

Alyona:

Sadly. Your jealousy is unfounded. Finding a girl who is not burdened with worries and personal life, who agrees to have sex with a married couple for the sake of interest, and on a regular basis, playing a supporting role, is possible only in a brothel. In normal life, free women still prefer traditional sex, in which a woman feels like a queen, and not one of two concubines, especially the "second" in status after the "beloved wife". So there is a chance that if there is such a hot young girl, then with secret thoughts to become not the second in the top three, but the first in the two. Basically, you're taking a risk.

What to do with it? Try to cause counter jealousy in her husband. A threesome is possible, after all, not only in the "two girls and one man" scenario. Offer him an experiment in reverse: find a call boy, and you watch how he and your boyfriend "do everything." And then join them third. Tell your lover that this YOUR experience is very one-sided and you would also like to be one with two, and not be "one of two" all the time. And defiantly start looking for a second man in your bed. Along the way, you can dream out loud, with your loved one, about what a wonderful experience it will be, try to copulate with another in his presence, how interesting it will be to compare the sensations of sex with one and the second, like at a tasting ... And so on. It is unlikely that your partner will like it, unless, of course, he is a complete pervert and not a secret bisexual.

Sergey:

Well, if you don't want to turn into a "narrow-minded bourgeois", then why stop? It is logical to expand the area of \u200b\u200bsexual education a little more and invite the guy to watch how some healthy man with a huge dick in front of him will rape you. Say you really want to experience it. By the way, maybe it is? Then you can find a couple of the same wide-eyed people and swap partners. It's also an interesting experience. And finally, after a series of such developmental activities, you will most likely find out that your boyfriend is very inferior in sexual education to some another partner, besides, he began to be jealous not like a child, and you will leave him. Maybe, of course, you won't find out and you won't quit, but it's still worth trying with another man in front of your own. Let him feel the way you do when he sees him having sex with another woman. It is quite possible that your sexual experiments will stop by themselves after that. Men for the most part, even very free-thinking, are very scrupulous about their partner.

You can afford anything and explain it with great love, but to allow the same for your girlfriend is for nothing. If you do this, you will see for yourself how he becomes gloomy and starts asking questions about who is better. And if a man also has a larger penis than your boyfriend, then it's completely kranty. Generally, in my opinion, such a breadth of sexual views and a strong family are two incompatible things. Because there are no limits to perfection. And everyone is free. And family is a limitation. Inevitable. Imagine that you have a child. There will be worries - more than enough. And in sex, the husband will have to refuse for some time. What will a friend like your boyfriend do? And when will it be necessary to play with the child instead of having fun in the bed? But he is still a young man, free, and in FIG he has such troubles? Are you afraid to be alone with your child? In short, in my opinion, you should stop, and immediately. Or then continue to bring the situation to complete absurdity. This is when your boyfriend says that you alone are not enough for him and now you will live in three, four. Well, and so on. Do you need it?

Inevitable. Imagine that you have a child. There will be worries - more than enough. And in sex, the husband will have to refuse for some time.

What will a friend like your boyfriend do? And when will it be necessary to play with the child instead of having fun in the bed? But he is still a young man, free, and in FIG he has such troubles? Are you afraid to be alone with your child? In short, in my opinion, you should stop, and immediately. Or then continue to bring the situation to complete absurdity. This is when your boyfriend says that you alone are not enough for him and now you will live in three, four. Well, and so on. Do you need it? Inevitable. Imagine that you have a child. There will be worries - more than enough. And in sex, the husband will have to refuse for some time. What will a friend like your boyfriend do? And when will it be necessary to play with the child instead of having fun in the bed? But he is still a young man, free, and in FIG he has such troubles? Are you afraid to be alone with your child? In short, in my opinion, you should stop, and immediately.

Or then continue to bring the situation to complete absurdity. This is when your boyfriend says that you alone are not enough for him and now you will live in three, four. Well, and so on. Do you need it? To have fun in bed, to play with a child? But he is still a young man, free, and in FIG he has such troubles? Are you afraid to be alone with your child? In short, in my opinion, you should stop, and immediately. Or then continue to bring the situation to complete absurdity.

This is when your boyfriend says that you alone are not enough for him and now you will live in three, four. Well, and so on. Do you need it? To have fun in bed, to play with a child? But he is still a young man, free, and in FIG he has such troubles? Are you afraid to be alone with your child? In short, in my opinion, you should stop, and immediately. Or then continue to bring the situation to complete absurdity. This is when your boyfriend says that you alone are not enough for him and now you will live in three, four. Well, and so on. Do you need it?

And again, there are many questions.

– *Will I like it?*

Guessing is useless until you try. It is better to choose a person you trust, who is physically attractive and likes both.

– *Where can I find the third one?*

Given the strict requirements for how your partner should be, the task seems overwhelming. Immediately discard the thought of a prostitute or the first person you meet from the Internet. Oddly enough, in fact, there are a lot of single girls around you who dream of this kind of sex extreme. Especially if you are a physically attractive and interesting couple. Familiar ladies, invited to visit or met at a party, under a few glasses of something alcoholic, will playfully answer your insidious questions about threesome sex. Well, then drag it immediately to your place or arrange for later. To try something like this, to feel the attention of two attractive people at once, is the hidden dream of quite a few, no matter how surprising it may seem at first glance.

– *What should the three of us do?*

It is clear that it would be necessary to prepare and memorize a few suitable postures and ideas for spending time together. Especially try so that no one has time to get bored. It is best to drink a little and take an aphrodisiac, and if a man is left alone with two girls, he will have to try to please both. However, if the girls like each other, the matter may not reach the man at all. We'll see how it goes. Think about the intellectual program of the evening, so that no one leaves disappointed: movies, conversations, games.

– *What to do with jealousy?*

What to do? If it is, then, probably, do not start the experiment. Jealousy must be dealt with in advance. In fact, jealousy is a feeling of possessiveness, the result of insecurity in yourself and your partner that he will stay with you for a long time. If you are sure of his love, that he appreciates you, if you want to share new feelings with him, then there should be no jealousy. However, it still occurs in the process.

– *What could be the consequences?*

The most varied and unpredictable. You may not like it and stop practicing it. You may not like it, and you will quarrel completely. You may like it, but fame will overtake you and acquaintances will arrange ostracism for you (they will avoid it, start a sea of rumors, and arrange a reprimand with putting it on the Internet). Or will you start caring together girls or boys.

Dreams must be brought to life. But better without a husband. The consequences may not please you, and especially him.

Lola

I promoted my girlfriend for a threesome the other day... Yes, it's fun to have sex with two beautiful girls. But the next morning there was a scandal ... My girlfriend began to be jealous.

Zorg, Donetsk

A threesome with my husband and girlfriend ruined my family.

Former

I had such a story, the former MCH tried to promote a threesome with another girl. He untwisted in the end, but the girl and I liked being together so much that we kicked him out of bed, or rather, he became superfluous. Ha-ha.

After that, he was left with a feeling of resentment, jealousy, envy and complete physical Unsuitability.

But these are his problems - and we discovered a new source of pleasure in ourselves :-))

Rima

My common-law husband and I also tried a threesome: M + 2F. Then he wanted to have a man: F+2M. And then this man brought his girlfriend - she is the first time: absolutely delighted! Okay, okay... There was no jealousy. The next day I went all in erotic excitement. But don't do it too often, it should be like a holiday! And most importantly, good people should be caught: cleanliness + you also need to talk about something! :-)

Zeta, Estonia

Some do not stop at the thought of threesomes and are carried away by the exciting idea of sharing all the joys and sorrows among three people, increasing the family and the amount of love. Everyone in such a trio is loved by two at once, is it bad? No, the idea is great. If all three love each other and do not feel jealous. But in reality, one person still considers himself deprived of something. There are families that openly talk about their life: common children, household, it's even very convenient when there is someone to share the hardships with and share the innermost ... It's hard to judge how happy they are, but the question is: is it worth judging? Why not let people live as they please? Polygamy is semi-legal in most countries and causes a lot of gossip. But it's quite an honest form of family, much more honest than the situation when one man has a lot of mistresses, moreover, each has a child and each is waiting for this man to come to her for the New Year. Well, they would have lived in the same house, and celebrated the New Year together instead of wasting energy on worries and quarrels.

Let's remember such a pastime as swinging. The couple wants new sensations and goes to a special club, where "falling sin" reigns, that is, complete freedom of sexual activity. The concept of jealousy is leveled, moreover, in such couples, partners are excited by watching one of them have sex with another person. Empathy works, that is, the ability to empathize, to feel the same emotions as the beloved (beloved). If there is no such club nearby or you don't want to communicate with strangers, a familiar married couple will do. During a joint party with pleasant music and booze, people go to many things that seemed impossible to sober.

Is it a perversion?

I have a rather strange situation. I've been married for two years now, I'm satisfied with everything in my husband, except for his long business trips. And in spite of everything, I always wait for him, I never cheated on him. Until I met a girl. She turned my head, we started a tight relationship, and everything turned into sex. First together. Then she persuaded her husband to join, at first I was against it, but then I succumbed. And that's where it all started. This threesome and other entertainments overwhelmed me. I admitted to myself that I like it, moreover, I realized that I love women more than men ... I don't know how to live on, I love and respect my husband. Is it a perversion? Or is it ok?

Saniya, Almaty, 24 years old

Alyona:

You would decide who you love more - a husband or women. Somehow it doesn't fit together. In your case, most likely, a husband is just something more stable and understandable. After all, you won't live openly with another woman - neither relatives nor acquaintances will appreciate it. Moreover, if they found out about your preferences, you would have to dramatically and radically change your environment. After all, not everyone can tolerate people with non-traditional preferences in sex. Whether this is normal or not is debatable. If it so happened that you love a person of your gender, then so be it. But it is love, and not the thirst for sexual entertainment in a different way that makes homosexual relationships worthy of respect (if not understanding, then acceptance). And when a bored woman meets her girlfriends,

I think you need to analyze your life and understand how else you could diversify it so that sex with aunts and their husbands is not the most vivid impression in your life. I am sure that this is precisely the problem - in idleness and lack of attention from her husband. These are the issues that need to be worked on.

Sergey:

Is it a perversion? In my opinion, yes. And although I am much calmer about female homosexuality than male homosexuality, I still think that this is not normal. As for how to live on, I think there are several options. Just let's make a reservation right away that there is no love for her husband at all. Respect - well, maybe to some extent. Attachment and some tenderness as to one's own - yes. But basically it's just dependence and unwillingness to lose a warm place, because it's supposed to be married, and here the person seems to be not bad, and earns money, and relatives don't bother ... So there is no love here.

Option one - divorce your husband and go into "entertainment" with your head. In my opinion, this is the most honest way out. In this case, of course, a scandal and a shameful exile cannot be avoided, but then you will have the opportunity to play enough sensations and find a person from whom you don't want to go "to the left". Option two - keep quiet in a rag and continue to amuse yourself with all sorts of perversions, while your husband earns money. Of course, everything can open up at one fine moment, and then see the first point, but it can also give a ride, especially if you don't roam right and left too obviously. It even has its advantages. After all, men almost never even think that the warm relationship of their wives with girlfriends is based on something much more than just general shopping trips. So if you exclude strangers from orgies and find a permanent partner without unnecessary jumps, then the wolves will be fed, and the sheep, or rather, the rams, will not guess anything. The third option follows, so to speak, from the second. Connect your husband to your lesbian pleasures. I think that a lot of men, and especially eastern people, will only be happy with such an option. True, with the involvement other men will have to be completely tied up, but you don't really need them anyway, and you can tolerate a husband. Here you are in chocolate, and the husband is in complete pleasure. After all, your husband may like your partner so much, and she likes him so much that they can jointly decide to exclude you from the glorious trinity. Well, there's nothing you can do about it. Risk is a noble cause. In general, keep it up.

Chapter 6

"Free love" or "free love" is a phrase that surely evokes in your memory images of barefoot long-haired people in colorful T-shirts and ripped jeans - hippies, a living symbol of the era of sex, drugs and rock and roll. The sixties really brought many people liberation from all sorts of moral restrictions, they became a time of struggle with the foundations that had developed over decades, if not centuries. But even with the decline of the hippie era, "free love" did not go away, except that, as the freedom of private life (caused by the same hippies) grew, it became not the lot of a few radical pacifists, but, although not too advertised, but not particularly condemned, a way to diversify one's own sex life for ordinary people that we see in our lives every day.

R. Heinlein became an apologist for hippie ideas. I will quote a few lines from his novel

"Stranger in a Foreign Land" about how a boy raised by Martians returned to Earth and learned love here, reversing her understanding in his own way. Here is what he says at the end of the novel: "The union of a man and a woman should not happen without love, but nevertheless it happens very often. Violence or seduction occurs - a game like roulette, only more dishonorable. And then prostitution, loneliness -

voluntary and forced - fear, guilt, hatred; children who grow up in the belief that sex is something bad, shameful, an animal. The greatest value that humanity possesses is distorted, perverted and presented as the greatest evil. The reason for this is jealousy. I couldn't believe it for a long time. Jubal, I still don't fully understand jealousy, it seems crazy to me.

When I first experienced love ecstasy, my first impulse was to share it with all the brothers at once: with women directly, and with men through women. I would be horrified if I were offered to take all the happiness for myself. At the same time, it never occurred to me to experience this joy with someone with whom I had not yet become related. I am physically incapable of loving a woman with whom I have not shared water. I am not alone: no one in the Nest experiences physical love unless they experience spiritual love. And here is the reaction of his interlocutor: "Jumble thought gloomily that only angels could live according to such an ideal scheme." This is roughly how the disputes between the ideologists of "free love" and their opponents took place. Ideas are great, but people are not angels. And we are driven by base instincts, which we strive to ennoble because of our humanity. And the logic of the development of society does not allow all people to remain equal, since their abilities and aspirations are very different. In general, philosophy is philosophy, and who will feed the children who are born? "Free love" also implies that further responsibilities for raising and providing for children - a heavy burden - should fall on someone else, and hippies will continue their political, creative, philosophical actions, disputes, games.

It must be said that free love is by no means something innovative and belonging exclusively to the second half of the twentieth century. Except for a few libertines, practically no one dared to challenge the correctness of the moralists. However, sexual relations at almost all times were completely free, but mostly not for women (a man in almost all societies could quite officially and unrestrictedly have a mistress, often more than one, while for a woman any affair on the side was considered a shameful fact as for herself and for her "cuckold" husband), and in the twentieth century the right to change sexual partners without powerful public censure was gradually acquired by women.

Young men like to proclaim the concept of “free love” until they truly fall in love and begin to be jealous of their passion for every lamppost. Until then, they are happy to lay out the basic concept of "free love": love should be given to everyone, to whom you want, when you want. And no obligations and restrictions! Only a sense of pleasure to be guided by. You can live in threes, fives, in a large commune, exchange partners and love everyone equally strongly. Feeling of ownership is better to put aside in the far corner of consciousness. This concept is used with pleasure by those who still do not want to settle down, and a beautiful phrase allows you to fool others.

Free relations

Help to understand the situation. I cannot understand anything ... I have a man who comes to me in order to make love to me. "I came, I saw, I conquered!" We feel good together! We are drawn to each other. But the matter does not go further than an intimate plan: an open relationship, without obligations and vows of love. I like him very much! Yes, and I told him too ... We are free. I am not married, he is not married. I just want to know how he treats me. I understand that there are no obligations ... But somehow I don't dare to ask him a question "about us". At first, such relationships suited me, but now he has somehow become closer, more expensive! I feel like I'm just being used, and it's so unpleasant ... It's just disgusting to feel like an "object of use." Or maybe it's not like that at all. Look into a person's head and read his thoughts! How to be, tell me ... How to act? Maybe.

Elena, Russia, 33 years old

Alyona:

And why such difficulties with checks? Are you not talking at all? Is everything happening silently? Are you already in a closer relationship, and are you embarrassed to ask the man with whom you regularly have sex about what he really plans for you? Or are you afraid that by asking a serious question, you will even lose your sexual partner? Well, decide what is more important for you: to have a permanent man for sex or still find a man who would like to start a family with you? After all, while you are dating this person, you are denying yourself the opportunity to establish other, perhaps more effective relationships than now. Or maybe your current man just doesn't understand that you need more than intimate meetings, that's why he behaves like that. You won't know until you're honest. But of course, be prepared for a response like:

"Are we bad together now?" - That is, to evade a real answer. Then you should think about who he holds you for. And about whether you really know everything about him.

Sergey:

If you just wanted to know how a person treats you, you would ask. In this case, there is a desire not just to get information, but to hear a specific, pre-desired answer. And even better - immediately offer. Is not it? Only here is hardly a man ready for this. After all, if he felt for you more than just sympathy and physical desire, then he himself would be looking for not only duvet meetings. So I don't think that anything big and bright will grow out of this particular novel. Although life is a big and complicated thing. Everything happens in it.

Be that as it may, your former "free" relationship is coming to an end. But what they will be reborn into, no one can say for sure. In principle, you can speed up the process by simply talking frankly. This is the easiest and most reliable way to arrange dots over "You". You are adults and understand everything perfectly. But you do not want this, because you feel that there can be only one point, and without "You". But if so, why try to "teach a lesson" or "test"? Much more hassle, but the result is the same. Although you can try to start to stop letting the young man into your home. Say that relatives have arrived or a girlfriend, or find some reason. After all, now it turns out that everything is simple for a man. There is a woman who is always ready “give”, and for this she has both the desire and the living space. Well, why bother?

So make him think about where you meet. Let him start bringing at least something other than a bottle of wine and a few milliliters of a cloudy white liquid. By the way, it's better if your sexodrome relocates to it. That is if he is not actually married. And then after all anything happens. He can say anything to you, but in fact, at home, seven are jumping on the benches, waiting for a folder to go home. In general, start breaking the existing system. Let complexities and ambiguities begin to appear in your relationship. Take a look at his reaction. If the guy becomes too lazy to invent something himself and he offers to reschedule meetings for a time when your “hut” is free, then it’s better to end the relationship. Although personally, I would prefer to just talk frankly on neutral territory. In a restaurant, for example, or on a walk. And easier, and ultimately cheaper.

The man who walks by himself...

I had such a family situation: after the wedding, my husband and I lived for six months, we had a child, and I started having serious health problems, my husband, unable to withstand all this, left and moved to another city. He occasionally came to my daughter and me, called. So we lived for three years. After three years, he decided to come back and try to live with us. We lived a year of normal family life. Now he is in frustrated feelings, he decided to leave again under the pretext that he needs to think and he can't find a normal job in our city. We have known each other since college, and our feelings have always been mutual. In another city, he has a child who appeared in these three years. But he's not going there either. I don't know what to do with all this. How to do it right?

Natalia, Kyiv, 24 years old

Alyona:

I think that the most correct thing in this case is to start building your own life, without taking into account the interests of a certain man who mistakenly turned out to be your husband. But the husband came out of him very nominal. It seems like it is, but there is zero sense from it. Here, operating on this zero, and begin to change your own life. Alas, this often happens: the birth of a child is not a link between a man and a woman, but a very serious test for lice, for the seriousness of the relationship, for the sincerity of feelings. Your husband has failed this test, twice already. He does not know how to take responsibility for the consequences of his actions. I tried - when I married you "on the fly", but I could not be noble to the end, I ran away. And from the second one, who bore him a child after you, he also fled. I ran away to you just then, as I understand it, when the one, the second, he was most needed precisely as help and support. In my opinion, to live with this is not to respect yourself.

So if you need advice, then here it is: let him “live and think” anywhere, but at the same time file for divorce yourself and feel like a free young woman who still has enough chances to meet a normal man, and not this ... something.

Sergey:

In my opinion, the most correct thing would be to start living anew, and leave the current husband in the past. You see, people are all different and each of us has a different attitude to what is happening. But each of us really needs a person who can be trusted, who can be relied on. Your husband has already betrayed you once, leaving you with a small child. Then he did the same to another woman, and now he's about to leave you again. What else should he do to make you understand that this person cannot be relied upon for anything? Can't you see that he doesn't need you, or your child, or that other family? He lives in his own "well" and the only person your husband truly loves is himself. Therefore, hoping for something good in the future with such a person is simply stupid. So why continue this whole circus? You're just wasting time and wasting nerves. He's not worth it.

"Free love" is not so bad: the idea is interesting, the embodiment - how it turns out. The most valuable thing about this idea is that people really need more freedom in love: so that no one forces them to it, does not force them to express their feelings indirectly or directly. It can be argued that now people are doing God knows what with their lives, changing partners, getting entangled in them, not knowing who their child is from ... But it's up to everyone how to handle the gift of freedom: accept, use for good or harm, throw away gift to someone else...

The concept of "free love" can also include such a moment: to love a person not for something specific, not in the hope that he will conclude a social contract (marriage) with you and will provide, not choose him on the principle of similarity with a certain ideal, but simply because you have common interests, there is sympathy for each other. And it doesn't really matter what gender he is if you are not going to implement a program to increase the birth rate. When at gay parades people shout loudly about their belonging to sexual minorities, they show that they have again chosen a certain limiter and will not let a person of the wrong orientation into their hearts. And "free love" is a combination of Christian all-forgiving love, the teachings of the "Tolstoyites" and many other teachings that proclaim love for all people at once. Only "free love also carries a shade of freedom of carnal love.

Alas, beautiful stories like "Emmanuelle" (this book proclaims many theses of "free love", in addition to specific examples, which is why it became a bestseller in its time) crashed into harsh reality. Bohemia has been knocked down by AIDS, people are constantly faced with sexually transmitted diseases, the best prevention of which is monogamy, and there is a risk of unintentional conception, despite all modern contraceptives. Random adventures often cause melancholy, the syndrome of loneliness swept megacities, and love for abstract humanity turned out to be easier than love for specific people. Indeed, in fact, love requires mental effort, not everyone can support the other not only in joy, but also in trouble, and even just in everyday life.

He loves two, but what about me?

I can't decide what to do, how to continue to live. My common-law husband and I lived for 4.5 years. We have a child, 3.5 years old. Over the years, I had to go through a couple of breakups with my husband (he left when I was pregnant and when the child was six months old). As he said, he left to sort himself out. Three months ago, I found out that he has another woman, and this is his "ex" before me. And he went not to think, but to her. She also has a child from him, 1.5 years old. When I found out, I made a scandal. And she told him to choose: either I or she. He did not think for a long time, and on the same evening, having previously called and called her to my house, he chose her. But that same evening he came back to me and said that he loves me and cannot live without me that he also loves her and cannot choose.

A month later, he offered to go to the registry office, but on the appointed day he backed out, that he told her that he wanted to leave me. And he told me the same thing, but in reverse. Another scandal. He asked for time to sort things out. Said he wanted to live with me. Time goes by but nothing changes. Recently, I said that I know that he goes to her, and not only to see the child. He replied that his child was there, that he loved him and was not going to leave him. Maybe I'm pushing him too hard, not giving him time to decide? I love him. But it can't go on like this anymore! And how to be further?

Maria, Russia, 23 years old

Alyona:

Your roommate is a young dunce. You and your opponent can flatter yourself that he loves both of you and simply "can't choose." In fact, he does not want to choose anyone at all. And it's not that you are both very dear to him and he cannot decide which of the mothers of his children to retire. He basically does not want to choose anything. He is 20 years old, he is not ready to finally decide and become a family man. For him, the birth of children was not the most desirable event - it was not for nothing that he ran away from pregnant cohabitants, "to understand himself." So I can assume that when a guy finally marries, then neither you nor the other one will be his wife. Neither you nor she are good enough for him to make a choice in someone's favor. A third one will appear, that she will not live with him out of wedlock and will not give birth to children at a fast pace to bind him to herself with this, but who will know her worth and whom he will be afraid of losing so much that he will run with her to the registry office. It's only a matter of time. While he was still young and satisfied with what he had, until the two of you found out about each other and started issuing ultimatums.

What should you do in this case? Don't know. Any advice will not be useful until you yourself understand that you have connected your life with a man who does not see you as a woman with whom he would like to live happily ever after until the end of his days. At 23, it's not too late to start over from scratch, even with a small child. But you will hope to the last that you are lucky with your current roommate, right? But which will know it's worth and which he will be afraid to lose so much that he himself will run with her to the registry office. It's only a matter of time. While he was still young and satisfied with what he had, until the two of you found out about each other and started issuing ultimatums. What should you do in this case? Don't know. Any advice will not be useful until you yourself understand that you have connected your life with a man who does not see you as a woman with whom he would like to live happily ever after until the end of his days. At 23, it's not too late to start over from scratch, even with a small child. But you will hope to the last that you are lucky with your current roommate, right? But which will know its worth and which he will be afraid to lose so much that he himself will run with her to the registry office.

It's only a matter of time. While he was still young and satisfied with what he had, until the two of you found out about each other and started issuing ultimatums. What should you do in this case? Don't know. Any advice will not be useful until you yourself understand that you have connected your life with a man who does not see you as a woman with whom he would like to live happily ever after until the end of his days. At 23, it's not too late to start over from scratch, even with a small child. But you will hope to the last that you are lucky with your current roommate, right? Until you both found out about each other and started issuing ultimatums. What should you do in this case? Don't know. Any advice will not be useful until you yourself understand that you have connected your life with a man who does not see you as a woman with whom he would like to live happily ever after until the end of his days. At 23, it's not too late to start over from scratch, even with a small child. But you will hope to the last that you are lucky with your current roommate, right? Until you both found out about each other and started issuing ultimatums. What should you do in this case? Don't know. Any advice will not be useful until you yourself understand that you have connected your life with a man who does not see you as a woman with whom he would like to live happily ever after until the end of his days. At 23, it's not too late to start over from scratch, even with a small child. But you will hope to the last that you are lucky with your current roommate, right?

Sergey:

As far as I'm concerned, nothing will change in your life. You are too young, gullible, do not have enough life experience, and pride is at zero. Your opponent is most likely the same, so the guy powders your head for both of you. You both think that he really loves one of you, he just can't choose. And explaining to you that this is nonsense does not make sense. When a person believes in something, it is very difficult to convince him. So for now, everything will remain as it is. Especially now you also have a purely sporting interest. After all, there is a “supposedly” rival, and therefore, by “winning” the fight for a man from her, you will receive confirmation that you are better. And the fact that everything is the other way around and the one that sends the walker faster than this will win is useless to explain to both of you. So how long will you play this game - I do not know.

Maybe, until someone gets bored. Personally, I think it's better to forget about this young man altogether. And if the guy is already entered on the birth certificate as a father, then it is better to go the official way and hang alimony on him. From a black sheep, as they say, at least a tuft of wool. And waiting for him to choose one of you is completely pointless. Just believe. And even if your opponent turns out to be smarter and sends the guy away first, nothing good will shine for you. These guys have one, completely uncontested, true love - it's themselves. Therefore, the appearance of another passion is only a matter of time. But, unfortunately, neither you nor your girlfriend in misfortune will listen to the words now. And keep wasting time, nerves and health. In the end, everyone has their own fun. That it is better to forget about this young man altogether. And if the guy is already entered on the birth certificate as a father, then it is better to go the official way and hang alimony on him. From a black sheep, as they say, at least a tuft of wool. And waiting for him to choose one of you is completely pointless. Just believe. And even if your opponent turns out to be smarter and sends the guy away first, nothing good will shine for you.

These guys have one, completely uncontested, true love - it's themselves. Therefore, the appearance of another passion is only a matter of time. But, unfortunately, neither you nor your girlfriend in misfortune will listen to the words now. And keep wasting time, nerves and health. In the end, everyone has their own fun. That it is better to forget about this young man altogether. And if the guy is already entered on the birth certificate as a father, then it is better to go the official way and hang alimony on him. From a black sheep, as they say, at least a tuft of wool. And waiting for him to choose one of you is completely pointless. Just believe. And even if your opponent turns out to be smarter and sends the guy away first, nothing good will shine for you. These guys have one, completely uncontested, true love - it's themselves. Therefore, the appearance of another passion is only a matter of time. But, unfortunately, neither you nor your girlfriend in misfortune will listen to the words now. And keep wasting time, nerves and health. In the end, everyone has their own fun. it is better to go the official way and hang alimony on him. From a black sheep, as they say, at least a tuft of wool. And waiting for him to choose one of you is completely pointless. Just believe. And even if your opponent turns out to be smarter and sends the guy away first, nothing good will shine for you. These guys have one, completely uncontested, true love - it's themselves. Therefore, the appearance of another passion is only a matter of time. But, unfortunately, neither you nor your girlfriend in misfortune will listen to the words now. And keep wasting time, nerves and health. In the end, everyone has their own fun.

It is better to go the official way and hang alimony on him. From a black sheep, as they say, at least a tuft of wool. And waiting for him to choose one of you is completely pointless. Just believe. And even if your opponent turns out to be smarter and sends the guy away first, nothing good will shine for you. These guys have one, completely uncontested, true love - it's themselves. Therefore, the appearance of another passion is only a matter of time. But, unfortunately, neither you nor your girlfriend in misfortune will listen to the words now. And keep wasting time, nerves and health. In the end, everyone has their own fun. Nothing good is going to happen to you. These guys have one, completely uncontested, true love - it's themselves. Therefore, the appearance of another passion is only a matter of time. But, unfortunately, neither you nor your girlfriend in misfortune will listen to the words now. And keep wasting time, nerves and health. In the end, everyone has their own fun. Nothing good is going to happen to you. These guys have one, completely uncontested, true love - it's themselves. Therefore, the appearance of another passion is only a matter of time. But, unfortunately, neither you nor your girlfriend in misfortune will listen to the words now. And keep wasting time, nerves and health. In the end, everyone has their own fun.

What is free love and what forms does it take? One can recall an open marriage - the marriage of two people who live separately from each other and meet at will, discussing together everything that interests them, but not linking their lives as closely as is customary for the majority. Why not an open relationship? You don't need to take care of a man, cook for him, wash ... But there is also no pleasure from mutual help at any moment. It seems that there is no way to get bored with each other when living apart, but who will hear your joke and sympathize right now if you are separated by kilometers? In general, all this is individual, and if you like such a marriage, fine. If not, something needs to be done: either look for another man, or issue an ultimatum.

Insisted on the wedding and lives separately from me

I need an advice. I love a man 21 years older than me. He is divorced and lives alone. He appeared in my life during a divorce from my first husband, helped me settle in a new apartment. He said he loves, wants to give birth to a son, offered to get married. After the wedding, nothing has changed: we each lived our own lives, met on weekends, and when we parted and went to our apartments, I suffered alone and did not understand: do we have a family? I saw no obstacles to living together, and when I tried to talk, he evaded answering. I got an explanation from him, and he said that he was not sure of me, that I would become his support in old age. No, I didn't cheat and didn't give reasons. I'm just emotional and impulsive, and he is calm and tough. I am raising a daughter from my first marriage for nine years, and we have an equal relationship with her, and he is an adherent of house building and is very strict with her. He said there was nothing to love about my daughter.

I set him a condition: we must live together, we are a family. And he left such obligations and made it clear that it is better for us to live separately, my daughter and I have our own arranged life, and sometimes he needs to rest. There is no mention of a son. He offered me to live like this, but I can't do it anymore. This semi-living together has been going on for more than two years, and I don't know if I'm married. I can’t use him to help around the house, for me he is a husband, not a lover. I love him, I consider him my husband, and I got married in the church! I understand I have to leave. And I suffer and wait for him to come and we will live happily ever after. My daughter and I have our own arranged life, but sometimes he needs to rest.

There is no mention of a son. He offered me to live like this, but I can't do it anymore. This semi-living together has been going on for more than two years, and I don't know if I'm married. I can’t use him to help around the house, for me he is a husband, not a lover. I love him, I consider him my husband, I got married in the church! I understand I have to leave. And I suffer and wait for him to come and we will live happily ever after. My daughter and I have our own arranged life, but sometimes he needs to rest. There is no mention of a son. He offered me to live like this, but I can't do it anymore. This semi-living together has been going on for more than two years, and I don't know if I'm married. I can't use him to help around the house, for me he is a husband, not a lover. I love him, I consider him my husband, and I got married in the church! I understand I have to leave. And I suffer and wait for him to come and we will live happily ever af*ter.*

Alyona:

Tell me why you got married? You are both unbelievers! In the Orthodox faith, the family is sacred. Have you even opened the Bible? Do you remember what is written there? What about the words of Christ: "... therefore a man will leave his father and mother and cleave to his wife, and the two will become one sheaf, so that they are no longer two, but one flesh. So what God has joined together, let no man separate..."? What are these games of guest marriage in the presence of a church marriage? I'm afraid that in your case, the wedding was only a whim of an aging peasant. He tied a young woman to himself by a rather serious act and continues to use her at his own discretion. If there were a believer, he would not behave like this, but would live as befits an Orthodox person - together with his wife.

The problem is that, in conscience, now if you divorce him, then through the church, and this is a very difficult path. Moreover, it makes sense to talk about this with the confessor and explain that not you, but your husband does not want to fulfill his marital duty and does not want to live a normal family. And if you spit on a church marriage and pretend that it didn't exist, since they don't put a stamp on your passport, then this is again a question of spirituality and faith. For me, a wedding is the very act that is better to postpone for old age, if both are not sure that they are ready to live a century together ... And now people get married - that they run to a beer stall, and there are no more thoughts about the responsibility of this step Your husband was not brought up in Domostroy traditions, but in the de Mostroy Soviet of Deputies. Neither one normal person in his right mind would not tell a mother that her child "is nothing to love." Is your maternal instinct completely killed by sex? How can you even listen to someone say that about your nine-year-old daughter? How can you think about having children from him and longing for him to live with you? What will your girl's life turn into when this "daddy" moves to you for permanent residence? And what kind of woman, what kind of person will your daughter grow up to be, if the idea is imposed on her from childhood that there is nothing to love her for? You know, maybe it's not something to love you for? If such statements do not shock you and do not cause protest, then, forgive me, what kind of mother are you? And how will you resolve the inevitable conflict between your daughter and this subject with whom you long to connect your life?

Sergey:

As far as I understand, the only thing that keeps you and this man now is that you got married. Or rather, not the fact itself, but the unwillingness to admit that it was a mistake. You stubbornly want to prove to yourself that he cannot be “not your” person, because you inspired yourself with the idea that he is yours. However, besides the fact that he helped you settle in the apartment and went to church with you, he brought nothing more positive, as I understand it, to your life. I would suggest that you sit down and think things through from the point of view of an adult. It is clear that you are an impulsive and emotional woman, but still. Nothing good has happened in over two years. Well, why then continue this circus? In general, in my opinion, every person lives and entertains himself to the extent of his own desires. I venture to guess that in fact, for some reason, you now need such an impossible relationship. Maybe you just want to suffer and suffer, maybe something else. Just keep in mind that while you are having fun in this way, your daughter, seeing everything that happens, is unlikely to experience positive emotions. Think about her. Personally, my view on this situation is as follows: send the uncle to where he came from, and build normal relations with a normal person.

The ideas of "free love" and free sex can be very beautifully described to everyone around, and in youth they excite the imagination. Moreover, they justify the desire to try sex with different guys and girls, without being distracted by doubts and moralizing. In addition to the obvious negative consequences, such as an unexpected pregnancy from an unloved person and

STDs (sexually transmitted diseases), there are hardly obvious ones related to the area of psychological experiences and interaction with society. These factors are not so obvious, they can be neglected, but this requires a certain amount of indifference and willpower.

First, no matter how a woman explains the principles of "free love" to herself and others, others can look at all this from their bell tower and put a label on her, give an unflattering definition of her behavior. And the men themselves, who seem to agree with you aloud and share your views, after having sex with you, they begin to advertise you to friends, invite you to a group sex, and discuss with all their friends. Alas, it is difficult to expect nobility from random fellow travelers of life, but they love to gossip and, most importantly, boast of their victories. Sometimes you have to change your place of residence if you need to find yourself a permanent man who would not hear about your adventures.

Secondly, a constant change of men is almost impossible if you spend a lot of emotions and time on each of them for communication, and then part. Too painful is the loss of a person with whom not only the body, but also life was shared, even if for a short time. And if you approach the matter without special feelings, just technically, then there is little pleasure from such promiscuity, since mechanical sex gives little sensation compared to sensual lovemaking.

Thirdly, it is rarely possible to remain friends with former lovers, and their new ones passions begin to hate you, as a rule, if you are nearby. In general, society constantly gets excited about such liberties on the part of a woman, while men are treated condescendingly, allowing them to "freely love" many women at the same time or in a row.

Slept with me on a recommendation

I got into a difficult situation that I can’t share even with my mother. I'm embarrassed to tell her about it. A year and a half ago I met a guy. He is five years older than me. I was his first woman. We went several times to his friend's apartment. And then he disappeared. I met a guy a month ago. He took care of me. We had several dates. He invited me to a cafe. Gave flowers. And the day before yesterday he invited me home. We had sex with him. But after that it turned out this! It turns out that this guy recommended me last year. And the current one said that I “none" in bed. Complete zero. Why am I writing? I need support because my heart is very disgusting. I'm afraid to be disappointed in men.

Belyanochka, Yaroslavl, 22 years old

Alyona:

I represent. In such a situation, sagging is the last thing. First, remember once and for all that a man who says about a woman that she is "a complete zero" in bed is almost certainly absolutely nothing of himself. Therefore, next time, directly answer such a statement that who would say, but not him, because you can consider what was sex with a very big stretch, so you didn't even want to try. Secondly, the guy who, after the first sex, reports that the girl disappointed him in bed, almost certainly didn't want anything else from her but sex. And it's not about you. It's about him. It's not you "some kind of not like that", it's "not right" with him. The guy had a specific desire pick up a girl for sex, he found out details about you from a friend and proceeded to bullshit. In fact, the same pickup truck, only easier to perform.

The only thing you need to change in your life is how you treat yourself. You act like a victim. That's why such garbage sticks to you. No need to cling to every guy who pays attention to you as if for the last chance, and no need to rush to transfer the relationship to a horizontal plane. Don't give them a reason to think that sex with you is a matter of several dates. Change something in your behavior. I don't know how, but the guys feel that this girl will agree to sex in order to continue the relationship. The main thing is that you learn to feel these guys. In general, it is a pity that you wrote little about yourself. Perhaps you should take up some kind of hobby that will help you expand your social circle, make new friends (judging by what you write here, you don't have friends with whom you could share your humiliation and find support). All in all.

Sergey:

But I think that it will be very useful for you to be disappointed in men for a while. And go study. Or work hard. And move away from mom. Start living independently, solving constantly arising problems. Take care of your daily bread, career growth, and much more. And get into difficult situations. And look for a way out of them. That is to grow up. Then, after a very short amount of time, you will begin to perceive everything that has happened in a completely different way. And the people around you will be different. For now, it seems to me that your childish naiveté is just a magnet for all sorts of gouging. Well, why did you suddenly decide that the first guy was the first woman? Because he told you so? And you immediately believed? And decided that with this you can go to bed? For some reason, I feel like it's the other way around. Not you with him, but he was your first. Some kind of nightmare. Until the age of 25, a man did not have a single woman? It's not even fantasy. It's something from mythology. Just think for yourself - what kind of bushy nerd do you have to be in order not to have sexual experience up to such an age? In general, let's grow up already. It would be time. And if for this you need to be disappointed in men, get disappointed quickly. Otherwise, until retirement, you will be upset over trifles and worry that you cannot tell your mother about something.

Chapter 7

We all hear about lofty things, we dream about love, we talk about it, we hope for high feelings ... But classic relationships still don't work out. And here you are confronted with the question: wait some more or act according to the principle "better tit in hand"? Indeed, in life there are so many halftones and shades, so many desires are unthinkable. Women are very fond of reflecting on the problem "Is it possible to be friends with a man without a hint of sex?" After all, two more important questions follow from this. First: can a man communicate with a woman disinterestedly, without secret attraction? And the second: is it possible to charm any man who is indifferent to you and "spin on sex"? Two sides of the same coin.

Everyone's experience is different, and someone can give examples of long-term disinterested friendship between a man and a woman, but I cannot find such examples. You can't look into everyone's soul, of course, but there are indirect signs: as soon as a girl has a permanent boyfriend, the rest of the "friends" who didn't hint at anything, didn't pretend, it would seem, but constantly talked and took for a walk, disappeared from the horizon. Platonic relationships with intellectual entertainment, philosophical conversations - everything suggested an exclusively asexual friendship, but all this happened only in the absence of other applicants. And "friends" - men began to entertain other girls. Large groups of boys and girls invariably fell into pairs or dispersed due to quarrels and mutual jealousy. The only strong friendly couples I've ever seen consisted of girls and guys of non-traditional orientation. In general, the interest of women in gays is surprising, but the fact is that many people love to make such friends and read fan fiction about homosexual couples. But certainly such men cannot be suspected of hidden erotic intentions. Although, again, this is just an illusion, because there are many bisexuals in the world who, under the pretext of their non-traditional orientation, manage to "touch" their "girlfriends", and they think that all this is "friendly".

Well, can't a man and a woman communicate without secret thoughts "in the wrong direction"? Somehow it even becomes sad ... And you can't trust a male friend, spend the night with him in difficult times? Perhaps this is possible, there are people of their word: they discussed the topic, closed it, no one bothers anyone. But still, most often it happens differently: friends at the moment of temptation find themselves in bed. And it's good if this happens by mutual consent, out of curiosity, etc. The confession of a victim of violence is posted on the Web, who tried to describe what happened in order to warn other naive girls. The bottom line is that a woman can confide in a friend with whom there has never been any flirting from her point of view, and when they are alone, he perceives this as an undisguised allusion to sex. And, despite the resistance, insists on his own, because "That's what you wanted, since you invited me to visit." No, this does not apply to all men without exception, but many simply do not understand the word "friendship", calling any relationship that way, including sex as a main bonus.

If mutual interest brought you and a friend to bed, then the friendship was just an old-fashioned courtship, and you did not know about it. Well, nice. If after this experiment you decide to continue on the terms of platonic communication, you need to understand the situation correctly: you didn't like it, and courtship stops. And in the best case, communication will continue. If mutual interest brought you and a friend to bed, then the friendship was just an old-fashioned courtship, and you did not know about it.

In general, think about this: is it possible to share friendship and love? If you look more broadly, it turns out that the concepts have a lot in common. What is friendship if not love for a person whom you are ready to help, with whom it is interesting and pleasant for you to communicate, to whom you are ready to give a lot? Only with a friend you will not sleep. What if you will? So this is true love? Or friendship plus sex, but minus obligations? After all, there is such a variant of modern friendship between a man and a woman: meetings with intimacy, communication, discussion of his mistresses and your lovers. You can call it friendship, or you can say its free love. There is no difference, the essence is the same. And finally, what is love, if not very, very close friendship? When feelings are stronger, when there is passion and sex is of great importance in your relationship. By the way, there is an opinion that between a man and a woman there can be either friendship or love. And it is ridiculous to combine this, that is, between lovers there cannot be trust of friendship, sincerity and other simple and important things, but they should be replaced by romance, courtship, dating rituals - everything is like in a movie. But still, the best love is a strong, faithful friendship, combined with passion. And how to call it is not so important.

We are friends who sleep with each other

We met a year and a half ago. Relations developed unstable, converged, parted. He is incredulous, if he sees a change in behavior, he concludes that the person either played before or is crazy. And I am emotional, and I was in love with him, so I reacted very painfully to all our disagreements. And he thought that I was cunning, trying to manipulate him. He is depressed, has almost no friends, it is difficult for people to communicate with him. He believes that the problem is in people, that he is very honest. He is critical of everything, criticizes me (I am a lawyer), because I am a clerk, a person who makes nothing out of nothing, who sells his soul to the devil. I considered him wise. I felt miserable. This led to fear. I tried to be interesting to him, but it only got worse, he felt that I was adjusting. He said that after intimacy with me, he had an emptiness in his soul.

He did not say that he loved, was not particularly interested in my life and did not talk much about his own. Over time, I realized that nothing good should be expected, and I decided to end this stupid relationship. I'm tired. In the New Year, we parted on ICQ. He admitted that he did not love me and did not plan anything serious. A month passed, he called. During this time, I got used to the idea that he is no longer with me. He said he was bored and wanted to talk. We met. From that moment began an incomprehensible relationship. We are friends who meet from time to time, watch movies, and sleep with each other. He likes. He believes it has never been so easy. What do you think? I'm tired. In the New Year, we parted on ICQ. He admitted that he did not love me and did not plan anything serious. A month passed, he called. During this time, I got used to the idea that he is no longer with me. He said he was bored and wanted to talk.

We met from that moment began an incomprehensible relationship. We are friends who meet from time to time, watch movies, and sleep with each other. He likes. He believes it has never been so easy. What do you think? I'm tired. In the New Year, we parted on ICQ. He admitted that he did not love me and did not plan anything serious. A month passed, he called. During this time, I got used to the idea that he is no longer with me. He said he was bored and wanted to talk. We met. From that moment began an incomprehensible relationship. We are friends who meet from time to time, watch movies, and sleep with each other. He likes. He believes it has never been so easy. What do you think? Sleep with each other. He likes. He believes it has never been so easy. What do you think? Sleep with each other. He likes. He believes it has never been so easy. What do you think?

Aya, Moscow, 26 years old

Alyona:

I think that if your childhood dream is to ruin your personal life, then you are closer than ever to your cherished goal. You are 26 years old, and all you pretend to be is the role of a girl for sex with a man who is incapable of close trusting relationships, love, and even, in general, friendship. Look at the situation from the outside: there is a man who periodically needs sex for health and maintenance of his tools. He has a woman he knows, lonely, unemployed, once in love and well-trained for a year and a half to suppress his own desires and self-esteem—simply trained to do what he needs, when he needs it. A woman does not demand anything in return: neither love, nor respect, nor, moreover, the obligation to "marry like an honest man." But, of course, she secretly hopes that since she is having sex, it means that at least she does not disdain, but at the maximum she still experiences some feelings.

Maybe he even loves somewhere, deep inside and there you never know - it will suddenly grow together, and there will be a Mendelssohn waltz, and a ring, and a dress! So this young woman lives the strange life of a free call girl for a man who doesn't give a damn about anyone but himself - so honest, smart and free. This woman has no personal life of her own. She has no chance to meet another man which would help her regain the lost sense of her feminine dignity. She has no chance to find a new love that will give her wings and faith in herself. She has no future as a loving wife and loving mother. And the worst thing is that she does not even resist her miserable position and does not understand that she is ruining her life with a man who has trampled on her dignity, and honor, and self-respect, and self-confidence. Sad picture, don't you agree? It's so mediocre to kill your life with a man who has never said "I love you" because he is very honest, and honestly says that you are shit that is only good for empty-headed, non-committal sex. And the worst thing is that she does not even resist her miserable position and does not understand that she is ruining her life with a man who has trampled on her dignity, and honor, and self-respect, and self-confidence.

Sad picture, don't you agree? It's so mediocre to kill your life with a man who has never said "I love you" because he is very honest, and honestly says that you are shit that is only good for empty-headed, non-committal sex. And the worst thing is that she does not even resist her miserable position and does not understand that she is ruining her life with a man who has trampled on her dignity, and honor, and self-respect, and self-confidence. Sad picture, don't you agree? It's so mediocre to kill your life with a man who has never said “I love you” because he is very honest, and honestly says that you are shit that is only good for empty-headed, non-committal sex.

Sergey:

The question, in fact, as I understand it, is about nothing. And to be honest, such questions are more like the emotional throwing of teenagers, and not a lawyer at the age of 26. But if everything is taken at face value, then personally I think that you are not yet the best lawyer. For, judging by what is written, she is notorious and dependent on the opinions of others. And your young man is an ordinary manipulator. Spoiled and hysterical. In addition, I believe that both of you are still learning the art of coexistence with other people. Therefore, there is no need to draw any global conclusions from what is happening. You're playing. And both of them love this game. Well, nice. Keep having fun. But, on the other hand, this process should not be delayed either. Life is a pretty short thing, even if it seems endless. And if you spend another ten years in such "incomprehensible" relationships, then problems may arise. Of course, if you, like a young person, think that periodically sleeping with each other after watching a movie is great, then for God's sake, continue. If you look at what is happening sensibly - such a relationship does not lead to anything.

It's just getting pleasure, and, as I think, only by a young man. Well, then why is all this necessary? Wouldn't it be better to suggest that the boy go look for another victim, and take care of his own life? Although if everything suits you so far, then who am I to interfere with adults? Ultimately, everyone is free to spoil his own life on his own. If you look at what is happening sensibly - such a relationship does not lead to anything. It's just getting pleasure, and, as I think, only by a young man. Well, then why is all this necessary? Wouldn't it be better to suggest that the boy go look for another victim, and take care of his own life? Although if everything suits you so far, then who am I to interfere with adults? Ultimately, everyone is free to spoil his own life on his own. If you look at what is happening sensibly - such a relationship does not lead to anything. It's just getting pleasure, and, as I think, only by a young man. Well, then why is all this necessary? Wouldn't it be better to suggest that the boy go look for another victim, and take care of his own life? Although if everything suits you so far, then who am I to interfere with adults? Ultimately, everyone is free to spoil his own life on his own.

Madly in love friend

I really want to get advice and hear your opinion about my situation. I have a friend, he is 22 years old. We've been friends for five years. They were always great friends, understood each other, and told each other everything that, for example, I would be ashamed and uncomfortable to ask my friends, the same thing on his part. I saw myself in him, and he saw himself in me. A year ago, I really wanted to kiss him. Our kiss smoothly turned into sex. After that, our friendship did not change, we also spent time together, had sex, but called it "friendship". We are together from morning to evening. In general, everything is the same as in normal couples, but we have friendship. I don't understand why we can't cross that line.

They laugh at us, they say we will get married, but we will argue that this is friendship. We say we love each other, but we say it like this: "I love you madly, FRIEND." I feel, deny. For example, he has friends (I'll call them that) - pronounced majors, for whom the girl who should be around is the one on the cover of the magazine. I'm not like this. With my height of 167, I weigh 57 kg. That is, when we walk with his friends, he listens to the opinion of everyone, and among them there is always someone who says something like: "With your appearance, you can find yourself a great girl." I love him madly and don't know how to tell him this. I know very well that I am dear to him, but what will be the reaction to my “I love you”, I don’t know, but to be honest, I’m very afraid that he will say that he can only be a friend.

Kira, Orenburg, 19 years old

Alyona:

Kira, what happens after you tell a guy: "I love you" - and in response you hear: "Let's remain friends!"? Will the war start? Will there be an earthquake? Will you lose your hands or your eyes? Really, tell me, why is the state of certainty worse than being in limbo? What is better to let the guy who plays "friendly sex" with you use your body, instead of getting rid of relationships that are unpromising for your personal future and give yourself a chance to find a serious partner?

In fact, what you are both doing right now is a game of feelings. You feel good together, but you are not yet ready, due to your age, to move to the next stage, so you came up with some kind of alibi for yourself: "We are just friends who sleep with each other." You, too, are not yet ready for more, otherwise you would behave differently. Just like your friend, you train by playing love, keeping a safe distance, leaving for yourself the opportunity to meet someone else tomorrow and, without much clarification of the relationship between you, start a serious relationship with these others. At least that's what happens to your friend. At 19, to want to be with a person of the opposite sex, it is not at all necessary to love him. It is enough to feel sympathy and common interests. The need for communication and manifestation of their sexuality - that's all that is needed. And love, you know she does not listen to the advice of friends, she does not care what other people think about her object.

Your boyfriend is still playing. You can continue to play along with him, but gradually you will get tired of it, and the relationship will no longer suit you completely. In my opinion, if just "friendship" with elements of sex with this person is not enough for you, it is better to tell him about it, and not wait for him to mature, if ever. You are not “not like that”, you are a normal girl who certainly deserves to be loved not for her appearance, but for other qualities. And what is important: you know how to love. So tell him about it. And if he thinks that you are not good enough for him, it is better to hear it now and take a time out. Perhaps after a while your relationship will resume, and on his initiative. It's not uncommon for such "friends" to blur their eyes, and in order to understand the significance of a particular person in your life, you need to move away from him for a while. That is, parting after such a relationship is not always the end. But you won't know if you don't try.

Sergey:

Kira, what is happening between you now, of course, can be called the first serious love or even love, no matter what you yourself say about this. And your relationship is real. However, unfortunately, most often the first relationship does not end like in a fairy tale. And this happens because you are still just learning to feel, love, build relationships. So far you are only training your independence, deciding on a place in life. You are still dependent on the opinions of other people, friends, and parents. You don't know a lot about life and about yourself, you don't understand how to react too many situations, you make mistakes, doubt, take offense and undeservedly offend other people. And there's nothing you can do about it. Alas, but a clear guide to teaching life has not yet been invented. You will have to learn how to solve problems yourself, fill own bumps. That is why the first relationship most often ends in parting, but is remembered for a lifetime. After all, this is a school. So in your relationship, most likely, after some time a crisis will come. You are already ready for serious steps in your life, you already want a family, and your boyfriend is still hanging out with friends and eschews responsibility.

Therefore, you are already experiencing dissatisfaction with your connection. And, alas, it will only grow. As a result, soon you will start to quarrel and eventually break up. Of course, this is just my opinion. And since everyone is different, your situation may be different. But this is what I have seen most of the time. Moreover, he himself went through all this. But what will happen next - no one can predict this. In my case, after a few months apart, my girlfriend and I realized that we still want to be together, and it will soon be 20 years since we have been married. However, the opposite also happens. What will happen in your couple, I do not know. It is very possible that you still part. But you shouldn't worry too much about this. Of course, now you think that this love is the only one and for the rest of your life. This is fine. Almost everyone your age thinks so. However, just believe me, this is a completely wrong opinion. As for your question about how to tell your partner that you love him, then history knows a lot of examples of the most insanely furnished declarations of love. Until the war. And the result is still the same. You just need to say these three words, no matter how scary for the consequences. However, the opposite also happens. What will happen in your couple, I do not know.

It is very possible that you still part. But you shouldn't worry too much about this. Of course, now you think that this love is the only one and for the rest of your life. This is fine. Almost everyone your age thinks so. However, just believe me, this is a completely wrong opinion. As for your question about how to tell your partner that you love him, then history knows a lot of examples of the most insanely furnished declarations of love. Until the war. And the result is still the same. You just need to say these three words, no matter how scary for the consequences. However, the opposite also happens. What will happen in your couple, I do not know. It is very possible that you still part. But you shouldn't worry too much about this. Of course, now you think that this love is the only one and for the rest of your life. This is fine.

Almost everyone your age thinks so. However, just believe me, this is a completely wrong opinion. As for your question about how to tell your partner that you love him, then history knows a lot of examples of the most insanely furnished declarations of love. Until the war. And the result is still the same. You just need to say these three words, no matter how scary for the consequences. That this love is one and only and for the rest of my life. This is fine. Almost everyone your age thinks so. However, just believe me, this is a completely wrong opinion. As for your question about how to tell your partner that you love him, then history knows a lot of examples of the most insanely furnished declarations of love. Until the war. And the result is still the same. You just need to say these three words, no matter how scary for the consequences. That this love is one and only and for the rest of my life. This is fine. Almost everyone your age thinks so. However, just believe me, this is a completely wrong opinion. As for your question about how to tell your partner that you love him, then history knows a lot of examples of the most insanely furnished declarations of love. Until the war. And the result is still the same. You just need to say these three words, no matter how scary for the consequences.

Let's be honest: how often does it happen that friendship is just a trick that allows a person to be close to the object of attention? You fall in love with a man who seems to be busy, or maybe everything will change at any moment, or maybe he will understand that you are so devoted, helpful, sociable, cheerful, always there - just what he needs. And you find reasons to communicate, say that you are friends, but hope, put on the best outfits, hint ... By the way, this is a good option to start a relationship. Friendship makes it possible to get to know each other better, to study a person from different angles, to claim sincerity on his part, because he has no need to show off and pretend in front of you. But reconcile yourself if, nevertheless, it never occurred to him to look at you somehow differently, with an interest far from platonic, even after a couple of years of constant meetings. No so no. Still, "chemistry" is also important, if there is no attraction of the body, is it worth regretting that it didn't work out your way? Not your person, then. And your pride has nothing to do with it. It is impossible to conquer everyone without exception and like everyone as a woman. Even your one-time victory in this case will turn into a defeat if a man, having not resisted once, nevertheless understands that you are not the heroine of his novel.

Friendship provides an opportunity to get to know each other better, to study a person from different angles.

Kissing and feeling nothing? I do not believe!

I have a friend who I like, I told him about it. Throughout the year, when he is drunk, we constantly kiss. And when sober, we pretend that nothing happened. But he doesn't want to meet ... He meets with everyone in a row, except for me ... He says that he feels that nothing will work out, I don't cling to him. Well, a person cannot constantly kiss the same one, not feeling anything, it seems to me ... I don't know what to do, I don't have any strength to look at his relationship with others ... And without him, nothing at all, feelings are closer to love.

Alexandra, St. Petersburg, 19 years old

Alyona:

Sasha, do not confuse animal instincts and human feelings (love, sympathy). The state of alcoholic intoxication does not expose the true feelings of a person, but removes social barriers, norms of behavior, morality and turns a person into an animal living by basic instincts. With a certain amount of alcohol and in the presence of a dark corner, you could already reach sex. Only it means absolutely nothing. A drunk man is just a drunk man. Sorry, but men even have a saying about how much you need to drink to kiss a woman or sleep with her, which you don't want to look at sober. Think for yourself - what could prevent this guy from having a sober relationship with you if you were interesting to him? Nothing. He is not bound by other girls, you are also free. That is, there are absolutely no obstacles for the two of you, if not for one "but": you "do not cling" to him.

He says it directly to you in exchange for your confession and is not afraid to scare you away, offend you, is not worried that you will stop loom near him, disappear, find another ... And are you still looking for some hidden meaning in his drunken hiccups? Don't be so cheap. This, by the way, is another possible reason why he is not interested in you when sober: there is nothing mysterious about you, nothing that you would like to discover, study, conquer. You are available and do not disdain any possibility of rapprochement with him.

Where a girl who knows her own worth and respects herself would be indignant, you happily answer drunken kisses. Well, who can a girl cling to with such behavior? "No way without him" is self-deception and lack of normal self-esteem. How to change this has already been said more than once. The most effective is to find yourself in some really interesting business, because this automatically brings about qualitative changes both inside you and in the people you communicate with. There are new acquaintances, new friends, and new goals in life. You look, and your object of sympathy will seem to you not at all as desirable as before. And what good can there be in a guy who drinks, doesn't know how to build long-term relationships with girls, constantly changes them and has all the makings for adultery in the future (the excuse will be the same: "I was drunk, I don't remember how everything turned out with Katya, Masha, Desha, Veronika Ivanovna ... because when sober, they don't catch me at all")? And your object of sympathy will seem to you not at all as desirable as before. And what good can there be in a guy who drinks, doesn't know how to build long-term relationships with girls, constantly changes them and has all the makings for adultery in the future (the excuse will be the same: “I was drunk, I don’t remember how everything turned out with Katya, Masha, Dasha, Veronika Ivanovna ... because when sober, they don’t catch me at all”)? And your object of sympathy will seem to you not at all as desirable as before. And what good can there be in a guy who drinks, doesn’t know how to build long-term relationships with girls, constantly changes them and has all the makings for adultery in the future (the excuse will be the same: “I was drunk, I don’t remember how everything turned out with Katya, Masha, Desha, Veronika Ivanovna ... because when sober, they don’t catch me at all”)?

Sergey:

Alexandra, if a guy doesn't want to date you, it means he doesn't want to date you. In addition, he openly says that you "do not cling" to him. What more confirmation of the absence of feelings do you need? The fact that a guy kisses you while drunk doesn't mean anything at all. Well, besides the fact that he is a novice alcoholic and in the near future will bring a lot of problems to himself and others. Just take my word for it that, being drunk, men can easily do a lot of other things that, having sobered up, they prefer not to remember. There is no mention of any love or increased sympathy here. You just turn under your arm, and a young man in a drunken stupor increases his self-esteem in such an unoriginal way. No more. And in the morning, having sobered up, he himself is probably surprised at what he did. That's why he pretends that nothing happened. And why do you need such a miracle? After all, not only is the guy already drinking, but also very promiscuous in relationships. Or do you just want to get into the "club" of his bedding for the sake of sports? Yes, and at least some kind of pride should be. After all, it is clear that this friend will not stop at any one girl. So do you really want to become “one of”, instead of looking for your boyfriend, for whom you will be the only one? No, if so, then continue. Someday your friend will get drunk to such an extent that he also manages to sleep with you. And you, which is quite possible, will become pregnant. And that's when the real problems begin. Unfortunately, in all likelihood, you still don’t even know what it is - the father of your child walking and drinking, who doesn’t need you or the child in FIG. Take my word for it - it's not fun at all. I really hope that the mind still takes its toll and you still send the guy to hell. Although, of course, to decide, of course, only you. In the end you old enough to be aware of his own actions. Then don't say you weren't warned.

How to start dating a friend?

I have a friend with whom we have been together for 7 years, and all this time we were just friends, and now we both realized that we want something more from each other, but only our desires differ in this: he wants intimacy, and I - a serious relationship ... When he offered to make love to me, I said that I would not be a one-night stand, and somehow hinted at a relationship, but he said that he was not ready for a serious relationship. After that, we still saw each other, kissed several times, but the problem is that I fell in love with him and can no longer communicate with him just as a friend, I can't just come up and hug him, I'm afraid that he will understand this ambiguously or think that I impose on him. What should I do so that he looks at me as a girl, and not a mistress, and is it possible for us to have a relationship with him?

Ekaterina, Ufa, 20 years old

Alyona:

You know, I had another question: why did you decide that if you, a 20-year-old girl, allow yourself to have your first sexual experience with a guy you have known for 7 years, then he will immediately leave you and you will be for him "girl for one night? No, of course, if you are sure that he will sleep with you and leave you, then, of course, this is not your option. But if this is said only for a red word and you experience mutual attraction to each other, then why not give free rein to your true feelings? I mean, why shouldn't two young people who are sexually attracted to each other, who are already hugging and kissing, afford more? Mom scolds? Or do you think that the one to whom you will surrender, as an honest person, will be obliged to marry you, otherwise it makes no sense to go to bed? And if in bed he turns out to be like this, that you have any desire to continue a relationship with him will disappear after the first time? How then to be?

In my opinion, you yourself may have scared the guy off by drawing a parallel between a love relationship and "serious intentions", which, as a rule, means starting a family. That's what a guy at 20 has the right to be "not ready." And if you really need a relationship with a registry office guarantee in exchange for sex with you, then this is not for him. But listen, why do you need a 20-year-old husband yourself? And if you really love him, allow yourself to love and enjoy it, and do not play the victim.

Sergey:

I think you yourself know the answer to your question. Although you and your young man have been talking for seven years, they are too different for something serious to happen. Different in outlook and age. He is still a boy who, even in a nightmare, does not see seriousness and responsibility, and you are already a young woman, trying on every man she meets for the role of husband and father. That's why you say you're in love. In fact this is not true. It's just that this particular young man was there for a long time, and when you grew up, your instincts first of all recorded him as the father of the family. This is completely normal. The feeling of being in love is exactly where it comes from. But at the same time, your common sense tells me that this is still quite “raw" material, which has yet to grow and grow to a real man. And that's great. This suggests that you are a person who primarily thinks with his head. Which means you don't do stupid things. So don't worry too much. Life itself will put everything in its place. I suppose you yourself will soon get tired of doing nonsense and your relations will change again. But this does not mean at all that in the future you will not be able to make a couple. Chances are small, of course, but they are. Only if this happens, it will be much later, when you are relatively equal in terms of maturity. Therefore, my answer to the question of whether you can have a serious relationship now is no. Even if you succumb to the desires of the guy, it will only accelerate the gap.

What to do if the friendship was "spoiled" by sudden sex, which left a feeling of awkwardness? Is it possible to save what is left, to forget what happened? Oh sure! No need to torture yourself in vain, life is huge, and there is so much in it that unsuccessful sex is just one of the little things, if you do not reflect for too long. Don't want to remember the mistake? Don't remember. Yes, there is the concept of “do not think about the white monkey”, when a person continues to think only about this, you need to take care of your personal life or other interesting things. Maybe this mistake will help you later choose guys for sex with great success. Well, remember that, for example, such an amount of wine leads you to rash decisions.

Another delicate question: is it possible to sleep with a friend just because there was no one suitable nearby, but you want sex? Honestly, the choice is yours. So what do you mean "can or can't"? It doesn't harm anyone around... Or are you afraid for your immortal soul? Are you vaguely afraid that you can't behave badly? Well, there may be consequences. For example, loss of respect for oneself and "friend". Since giving your body just to someone not out of love, but "because it's itch" is a little humiliating, don't you think? Again, time and energy are wasted on the wrong person, maybe this energy can be directed to more useful goals and interesting objects? But if you do not perceive it as a humiliation and respect your male friend, then why not? As long as you don't happen to conceive a new life from a person whom you consider only a temporary refuge from personal problems.

Friedrich Nietzsche expressed a wonderful idea: "Friendship between a man and a woman is possible ... with a certain amount of physical disgust." Perhaps so, but will a man be friends with someone who is unpleasant to him? Is that in the presence of common interests and goals, being colleagues?

We read the comments of those who were personally affected by the topic of a woman's sex with a male friend.

Guys usually make friends either with scary girls, and this is male friendship with all the consequences: what kind of women are fools, how to properly have sex and in what positions, obscene jokes, booze, talking about engines, computers, shooters, a hunting knife made of Damascus steel, and what kind of women do you like and so on, so on, so on ... And by the way, a girl no longer has the right to be a girl, she must know what an engine and 95th gasoline are, how a vidyukha is inserted and what an upgrade is, and look at it quite calmly in shorts and with beer.

Another is a girlfriend: there is a significant difference. He treats her like a woman (in every sense), but for some reason (more often this is the presence of a boyfriend, husband) he STILL DOES NOT SLEEP WITH HER. Either she rejects him, but he has the hope that she will someday understand that he is cooler than those goats about whom she often complains to him. After all, he does not offend her, he trusts her and she trusts him, he treats her with beer, wine, coffee ... He is good, but he is SO ALL GOOD AT ALL HER DOES NOT NEED. Rather, it is needed, but only as an assistant: to cry into a vest, fix an outlet, a car, and a computer, assemble or move a closet, dig up beds, etc.

Krasnoyarsk

I had such a story with my friend: his name was Sasha, we were friends, we were friends, and we were inseparable almost around the clock. As a result, he offered a closer relationship and this disappointed me very much!!! After all, I trusted him even the intimate details of my life! It turns out that he looked at me as the woman of his dreams, which I, in turn, did not feel for him!

Murlisenka

Is friendship possible between different sexes?

Of course, I agree with the opinion that such friendship is impossible. More precisely, it simply differs from normal friendship in its short duration (although it can last for years, but the end is predetermined), as well as deliberate insincerity (after all, recognition destroys it). I watched a lot of such "friendships", but they always ended like this:

1. Mutual recognition and sex love.

2. Recognition is one-sided, left unanswered, and the break is forever.

3. The more active one, the initiator of the cell, suddenly falls in love with someone else and disappears from the horizon suddenly and forever, during random meetings brings a blizzard and is always late somewhere.

Young women in these matters are generally prone to self-deception and realize their attraction (during this very pseudo-friendship) only when they start to go off scale, turning into love. Guys are less prone to self-deception, usually they just sigh and wait in these cases, although self-deception does occur. But sometimes young guys also deceive themselves, while being under some stress (subconscious fear of recognition, etc.).

The explanation for this phenomenon is very

simple: if a person of the opposite sex is sexually unattractive for you, then you will not be drawn to "be friends" with him, but if it is attractive, you yourself understand. Despite the fact that sticking your head in the sand wherever you get and pretending to be brooms, we all love it very much.

Maye sky, Warsaw

This topic has always been of great concern to me. And now, reading this article, I tried everything on myself. The fact is that for 6 and a half years I have been communicating with a person very dear to me, with my soul mate. We used to meet for about two years, then broke up, but we always maintained a very reverent and warm relationship, in general, we were friends, because we thought that this was an ideal option for the two of us. During this time, we both had various romances and even serious relationships with other people, but the bond between us (friendly!) always remained. And this summer, after I broke up with my last boyfriend, I had sex, we again ended up in the same bed with him ... I scolded myself for a long time, saying that it was only for consolation, I was afraid that our friendship would end there , but in fact I was hoping for a revival of relations! And what, everything remains the same, although I no longer need it! But the main thing - with him, I sec, something is also happening. I think we are just afraid of this relationship again, which is why we prefer to remain silent and hide everything behind the mask of friendship. BUT I'm tired of it, what should I do? How to talk to him?

And I already don't understand anything in our relationship ... We've been friends for a year now, and we sleep together, but we don't live under the same roof! He makes renovations in my kopeck piece, together every day (we solve mine, then we glue the wallpaper ...). When I once asked him what feelings he had for me, he replied: "Friendly", said that he did not love me, and sex with me was SUPER!!!

My God, what a vinaigrette! I demand urgently to separate the flies from the cutlets!

Once again I am convinced that the old man Sigmund Freud is right about the fact that everyone person's behavior is governed by his sexuality or libido.

And one of the great ones said that friendship between a man and a woman, as such, does not exist, it is either the beginning of love or its completion. Sex is not required at all.

Tamilla, Wilno

All this, of course, is very individual. For me, it is not difficult / torment to remain friends with a former lover. On the contrary: I know him much better then, and he knows me. We have nothing to be ashamed of before each other, because we know each other so well. And there are no more complexes left, communication is much easier and more trusting. But not everyone is like that, especially if the feelings of one have faded, and the other- No.

But if I sleep with one of my already existing friends, then, I'm afraid, it would be more difficult for me to clog these feelings back. But then again, this is different for everyone.

But about the possibility / impossibility of friendship in general between a woman and a man - then, of course, it is possible. I don't know what Nietzsche's problems were, but I don't think "disgust" is a necessary part of it. And then, what then to say about gays or lesbians? That the former cannot be friends with men, and the latter with women? And what then to say about bisexuals?? Why can't they have friends?

Am I really just a friend to him?

I have a good friend. We are interested together, many times we went to rest in the same company, we often go to the cinema with the same company, go skating, and we also celebrate all the holidays together. Moreover, he usually acts as the organizer, and, in his opinion, I should always be there ... “It's just that I'm used to having you around every holiday and every event,” he said to my refusal to go on a picnic. But he avoids being alone with me. We communicate very often on the net, he doesn’t leave me at work ... He respects me very much, often consults me. Take care of me. He hugs only when we take pictures (and he also loves to take pictures with me and then post it on a social network, then, after looking at the photo, friends ask: "Are you dating?"). Cares and is interested in my personal life. He even tried to set me up with his best friends. He has a girlfriend, he always tells me about her, I help him choose gifts for her ... I really like him, and I don't have feelings for him as a friend. But I can't figure out if he really thinks I'm just a friend? It's just that he devotes too much time to me, and sometimes it seems to me that he is simply afraid to confess to me and is afraid to take the relationship to another level ... I want to know your opinion: will a guy devote a lot of time to a girl if he just wants friendship?

Dina, Kazan, 23 years old

Alyona:

It is interesting to look at that girl who, with angelic patience, remains without a boyfriend for all the holidays, goes to the cinema alone, accompanies him to a bachelor's vacation in the company of other young girls, and then, obviously, with tenderness and pride, looks at photographs of her beloved, captured in an embrace with different, and the same girl. In general, something tells me that this "girl" is from the field of modern mythology. And if you are with a guy and buy gifts for someone, then most likely for your sister or some other close relative.

Why is he deceiving you? Well, it's probably easier for him to keep some semblance of distance. Perhaps he himself has not yet figured out what feelings he has for you and whether he wants to translate your friendly and non-binding relationship into a serious direction. Maybe he's afraid that if you get more rights to him, you'll stop being so sweet and understanding. There can be any number of reasons. He may simply consider that now he does not need a serious relationship, he may have plans for a career, development, which he cannot imagine how to combine with personal relationships. Well, for example, he may suspect that as soon as you move to a new stage, you will immediately want a veil and a ring, but he is not ready for this. Actually, probably "he is not yet ready for a serious relationship" is the most reasonable explanation for his behavior. He definitely likes you but for now he does not want to let anyone into his personal territory. And, probably, the main problem is that this game will continue until he realizes that he can lose you forever. Of course, if by then you will still be interested in him.

Sergey:

The fact that the guy is breathing unevenly towards you is for sure. No normal man will pay so much attention to a girl he doesn't like at all. And certainly photos with her will not be shown to everyone. Therefore, I believe, there is a basis for starting a relationship. I don't believe he has a girlfriend. I suppose you yourself understand that no sane woman will allow her man to go on holidays with the same constant girlfriend, and even more so put photos of her in an embrace for all to see. So the girl is most likely mythical. I hope the guy is really in love and is just a coward to transfer relationships into close ones. This is the most common option and the most likely. Alas, very often young people believe that such a wonderful girl will never be able to fall in love with someone like him. Especially if the lady is so smart and successful that you even have to consult with her in work matters.

So they jump around, push their tail, and when it comes down to it, they immediately go into the bushes, because it's scary to open up and hear a refusal. If so, then the only option is to catch the young man by this very tail or whatever else will hang out there and take the initiative into his own hands. Otherwise, the first steps, and even more so recognition, can be expected before retirement. In general, make a date with a guy and honestly lay out everything that you think and feel. If he is really in love, he will remember this conversation with gratitude all his life. If not, at least you won't have any more doubts. This is also good. Because it's scary to open up and hear a rejection. If so, then the only option is to catch the young man by this very tail or whatever else will hang out there and take the initiative into his own hands. Otherwise, the first steps, and even more so recognition, can be expected before retirement. In general, make a date with a guy and honestly lay out everything that you think and feel. If he is really in love, he will remember this conversation with gratitude all his life. If not, at least you won't have any more doubts. This is also good. Because it's scary to open up and hear a rejection.

If so, then the only option is to catch the young man by this very tail or whatever else will hang out there and take the initiative into his own hands. Otherwise, the first steps, and even more so recognition, can be expected before retirement. In general, make a date with a guy and honestly lay out everything that you think and feel. If he is really in love, he will remember this conversation with gratitude all his life. If not, at least you won't have any more doubts. This is also good. If he is really in love, he will remember this conversation with gratitude all his life. If not, at least you won't have any more doubts. This is also good. If he is really in love, he will remember this conversation with gratitude all his life. If not, at least you won't have any more doubts. This is also good.

Chapter 8

It would seem that virtual sex is an invention of recent years and only lonely teenagers need it ... But no! Let's dispel any illusions about this. First, what is virtual sex, if not sex at a distance, without personal contact? The modern version of the virtual is a continuation of intimacy by telephone, invented in the last century. Well, even earlier there were playful notes at the ball, drawings on the walls, transferring their portraits to each other in a frivolous form ... People's fantasy in the field of sex is truly limitless!

Now technical achievements open up even more opportunities for us: love correspondence via the Internet, SMS, ICQ, chat, Skype ... At any time of the day or night, without leaving your computer, or you can comfortably get into bed with your phone and ... Arrange a real night of passion with a familiar or not at all familiar partner, or even ... a robot. Yes, yes, the complication of intellectual programs that imitate human communication occurs daily, and the pattern of conversations on intimate topics is also quite monotonous. And there are also video chats, online rooms for virtual meetings with uninhibited young ladies. For money, you can chat with prostitutes on the Internet, but it is even more interesting to make acquaintance with real people, letting your imagination run wild and pretending that you are a cool macho or a gorgeous blonde with big breasts. No obligations, the ability to close the chat at any time and disappear forever from the interlocutor's field of vision give a feeling of freedom and impunity. You can play someone else, temporarily "change" gender, "correct" age and appearance.

Well, if everything develops into something serious, go to the real world and try something more. If this is not possible (due to the presence of a husband or wife, disability, etc.), then at least in this way to live a different life - in the virtual world.

She called up the mail program. There, messages from the previous week and this morning's letter were waiting for her. Without reading, she transferred them to the "deletion box".

I shouldn't be reading this. I decided so," she said aloud, as if giving herself an order.

She then dialed his address:Jakub@epost.de.

For the last time, she thought as she sent the e-mail. And I felt relieved. It's just the internet...

Then she opened the folder in which she kept all the emails she received from him. Gave the command to delete. The program learned:

"Are you sure you want to delete these messages? (Yes/No)" She sat motionless for a few seconds, staring at the screen.

"Stupid question!" she thought angrily.

And suddenly I felt as if someone's life depended on the answer to this stupid question.

Red or blue wire? If she cuts the wrong one, everything goes up in the air. Like in those stupid movies where a handsome, tanned semi-idiot always cuts "that" wire. She remembered that in no film, no one cut the red.The phone rang. Her husband drove up, he was waiting for her downstairs. She clicked "Yes". Nothing happened. The world has not fallen into turmoil. The audience breathed a sigh of relief.

She turned off the computer. Got up. She touched the monitor screen. The screen was still warm. Farewell Jacob...

She turned off the light and went out.

Janus Wisniewski. Loneliness on the Web

There are a huge number of people "hanging out" on dating sites now. More and more couples are talking about how they met online. And the myth that a serious relationship will not work out of online dating does not always find confirmation in real life. But communication on the Internet still has its own nuances. The fact is that the sincerity of the addressee is difficult to verify. And the question of trust is very acute, but the imagination completes what the interlocutor kept silent about. You can be in this ephemeral connection for years, share the most cherished with each other, living on different parts of the Earth, enjoy light flirting or passionate correspondence that lasts like a novel that you write together. But to build your life based on the letters on the screen, not knowing whether your virtual reality really wants to meet you.

“Lover”, whether you like him in reality, is like building a house on sand. Even fans know more about their idol than you do about your friend from the social network, since the "star" is constantly attacked by the press and its existence is documented. And a meeting with a prototype of an Internet image is always a serious test. However, the comparison with the fans did not come by chance: for years they cherish the hope of meeting, catching every word of the idol, in their imagination experiencing one romance after another with him, chasing him around cities and countries and really love not him, but the image created by them in their head. It is impossible to know a real person, having an idea only about his work, looking at his photographs and reading his interviews (verified phrases for publication). And love for an ideal image has little in common with love for a real, actually existing man. The same is true with virtual novels. Everyone wants to show themselves better than they really are, so we are dealing with an improved version of the person on the Web.

Is he using me as an internet application?

I want to share with you my experiences. It so happened that I met a guy on the Internet and fell in love with him. He also constantly tells me that he loves me, but sometimes it seems to me that he is mocking me. He can cut veins, swallow pills if we are in a quarrel. I understand that this is not normal, but to give up everything ... This does not fit in my head. We have been talking for 2.5 years, we live far from each other, it seems that everyone is against us. I became so attached to him, I don't even need anyone in reality, although I could already find something more serious. But in addition to all this, he has a best friend, to whom I am constantly jealous of him, at a distance it is hard to fully trust a person. Because of her, we constantly swear, argue, we cannot communicate for 3 days. But he says that she is a childhood friend, like a sister, and dear to him. Here's what I'm thinking: is it even worth believing a person whom I saw only in a photo, maybe it's all a hoax, I'm not the only one with him and in general he manipulates me or just uses me as an application on the Internet? Tell me please!

Olay, Moscow, 21 years old

Alyona:

I think it's time for you to use your brains. Well, they can't be idle for that long. How can you believe in all this nonsense? Do you really and seriously think that the guy cut your veins and swallowed pills for you? And he could, in his virtual fantasies, unsuccessfully hang himself, for example, or jump under a train, surviving (well, miraculously, the train turned at the last moment). With the same success, the guy could be a secret agent of Interpol or Mossad. He could be the illegitimate son of Prince Charles or the illegitimate son of Princess Diana. Whom she hid from the public ... Well, how can you trust a person whom you have never seen? And how can you even know that he lives very far from you? After all, it's all just words. He may even be your neighbor or just live on the other side of the city. How can you check it? After all, everything, absolutely everything that you know about him, all the information that is available to you, is only what he himself gives you. Your virtual may not be a young guy at all, have you thought about it? It could be a 50-year-old man who is your daddy age, or a 30-year-old lesbian, or a 15-year-old teenager who feels very cool because he managed to pick up an adult girl. In general, honestly, there are no words to express surprise at your naivety. How can you fall in love with a virtual? Well, if you lived in a small town, where, apart from the Internet, there is no one to communicate with ... who is your dad, or a 30-year-old lesbian, or a 15-year-old teenager who feels very cool because he managed to pick up an adult girl. In general, honestly, there are no words to express surprise at your naivety. How can you fall in love with a virtual? Well, if you lived in a small town, where, apart from the Internet, there is no one to communicate with ... who is your dad, or a 30-year-old lesbian, or a 15-year-old teenager who feels very cool because he managed to pick up an adult girl. In general, honestly, there are no words to express surprise at your naivety. How can you fall in love with a virtual? Well, if you lived in a small town, where, apart from the Internet, there is no one to communicate within general, my advice: tie up with Internet hallucinations. It will be a huge pity to find out in a few years that you were just a living Tamagotchi with some bored married man of about 40 or a jerk of about 16. And if you really want to check who your "beloved" really is, make him at least get out Skype video chat and prepare for him a series of test questions that only he could answer, and not his friend or son, who agreed to participate in the game. But, to be honest, fantasies about open veins and drunk pills alone would be enough for me to suspect a person of a violent fantasy and stop wasting time on him. You won't be 20 for the rest of your life.

Sergey:

I don't think falling in love with a dream is a bad thing. Such feelings also have a right to exist. They are good training before real relationships. It is clear that now everything is 90% invented. And about veins with pills, and about a girlfriend, and about everything else. You're playing. He gives you the feeling of having your man, one that you have not yet met in reality. You also give him something, otherwise your correspondence would not last so long. But all this will not last forever. Just believe. Sooner or later, both of you will grow up, and the "first sign" will be the desire to meet in reality. Most likely, this will be the beginning of the end for virtual love. Unfortunately, in reality and on the

Internet, people are usually very different. And therefore, personally, I think that you are unlikely to want to stay together. After all, a beautiful face in the photo does not move, does not go to the toilet, does not scatter his things anywhere, he does not smell from his mouth. And it is always available for conversation, does not linger at corporate parties, and does not come home drunk.

But the real person is just the opposite. No, of course, there are enough examples when virtual relationships turn into real ones and a family develops, but more often the other way around. There's just nothing wrong here. Just life, one way or another, will take its toll. Therefore, do not attach too much importance to your connection. If it is given to develop into something more, then so be it. Well, if not, then no. In general, most likely, everything will be fine, but not quite the way you are planning now. Of course, there are enough examples when virtual relationships turn into real ones and a family develops, but more often it is the other way around. There's just nothing wrong here. Just life, one way or another, will take its toll. Therefore, do not attach too much importance to your connection. If it is given to develop into something more, then so be it. Well, if not, then no.

In general, most likely, everything will be fine, but not quite the way you are planning now. Of course, there are enough examples when virtual relationships turn into real ones and a family develops, but more often it is the other way around. There's just nothing wrong here. Just life, one way or another, will take its toll. Therefore, do not attach too much importance to your connection. If it is given to develop into something more, then so be it. Well, if not, then no. In general, most likely, everything will be fine, but not quite the way you are planning now.

Moving to my virtual love

I met my man on the Internet, we talked for a long time, and then we began to call each other. He lives in another city. That's why we don't see each other often. We mostly talk on the phone for hours. I'm planning to move in with him in two months. The problem is that he was married and he has a daughter from his first marriage, I have a son, I am also divorced. His wife is now living with another man (but not married), expecting a child from him. But sometimes it seems to me that my young man still loves her, although he tells me that this is all in the past and that he loves only me. He says they are just friends. I am very afraid that he will return to her.

Maria, Saratov, 25 years old

Alyona:

Maria, there is an Old Russian saying: "If you're not sure, don't overtake." If you are not 100% sure of your man, you don't have to rush to him with suitcases, taking the child under your arm. At the very least, it's stupid. You have to be able to listen to your female intuition. If she tells you: "Something is wrong here," most likely, you really should listen to this "worm" inside yourself. Most of the ladies who ignore his voice then wring their hands and smear snot on their faces with exclamations: "I felt that it would be so!" In general, if you are afraid that your man still loves his ex-wife, do not rush to move in with him.

Virtual communication is virtual because it is very often far from reality.

There is another reason to take your time: you probably do not know everything about him. All you have is communication on the Internet and by phone. For those rare meetings, how much can you find out factual information about a person in order to decide to connect your fate with him and entrust him with your child? Virtual communication is virtual because it is very often far from reality. What is this person like in everyday life? What will he be "daddy" for someone else's child, if he could not become a good father to his own? And, perhaps most importantly: why did he divorce his wife, especially if he had a common child? Who will win quit? What was the reason? Someone might say that this should not concern you, but in my opinion these are fundamental issues. You are going to connect your life with a man who already has one unsuccessful experience of family relationships behind him. That is, this man already once created a family, but could not save it.

It doesn't really matter who dumped who. If he left his wife, then it means that he is not a very reliable life partner (leaving the mother of his child ...). And if the wife ran away from him, having captured the baby, how was it necessary to behave with her (women with small children go for divorce only in extreme cases)? In short, a divorced man is a dubious gift of fate to accept without further information. It's obvious that you don't know much about him. In my opinion, what you need to be afraid of is not that that your lover longs to reunite with his ex-wife, but that he will simply disappoint you when your virtual romance is replaced by everyday life. In my opinion, it would be better for you to start with a trip together on vacation, and the three of you, with your child, and not to an all-inclusive hotel, but somewhere "savages", where you would have to run around shopping and lunch (at least breakfast) to cook. So you'll see how he behaves with the child, how he reacts to attempts to involve him in solving everyday issues. Well, he will look at you and really appreciate his ability to accept a woman with someone else's child. After all, you have a mutual problem: he also has little idea of \u200b\u200bwhat it is like to live with you every day, and not just sharpen flies on the phone. When your virtual romance will be replaced by everyday life. In my opinion, it would be better for you to start with a trip together on vacation, and the three of you, with your child, and not to an all-inclusive hotel, but somewhere "savages", where you would have to run around shopping and lunch (at least breakfast) to cook.

So you'll see how he behaves with the child, how he reacts to attempts to involve him in solving everyday issues. Well, he will look at you and really appreciate his ability to accept a woman with someone else's child. After all, you have a mutual problem: he also has little idea of \u200b\u200bwhat it is like to live with you every day, and not just sharpen flies on the phone. When your virtual romance will be replaced by everyday life. In my opinion, it would be better for you to start with a trip together on vacation, and the three of you, with your child, and not to an all-inclusive hotel, but somewhere “savages”, where you would have to run around shopping and lunch (at least breakfast) to cook. So you'll see how he behaves with the child, how he reacts to attempts to involve him in solving everyday issues. Well, he will look at you and really appreciate his ability to accept a woman with someone else's child. After all, you have a mutual problem: he also has little idea of \u200b\u200bwhat it is like to live with you every day, and not just sharpen flies on the phone.

Where you would have to go shopping and cook dinner (at least breakfast). So you'll see how he behaves with the child, how he reacts to attempts to involve him in solving everyday issues. Well, he will look at you and really appreciate his ability to accept a woman with someone else's child. After all, you have a mutual problem: he also has little idea of \u200b\u200bwhat it is like to live with you every day, and not just sharpen flies on the phone. Where you would have to go shopping and cook dinner (at least breakfast). So you'll see how he behaves with the child, how he reacts to attempts to involve him in solving everyday issues. Well, he will look at you and really appreciate his ability to accept a woman with someone else's child. After all, you have a mutual problem: he also has little idea of \u200b\u200bwhat it is like to live with you every day, and not just sharpen flies on the phone.

A divorced man is a dubious gift of fate to accept without further information.

Sergey:

In my opinion, the possible presence or absence of feelings in your friend for his ex-wife is just one of the possible problems, and not yet the most important one. After all, if you are suitable for each other, if your relationship develops normally, then no former feelings for former partners will play a role. But you don't know each other yet. You just talk on the phone and occasionally meet. The fact that such communication is going well suggests that there are chances, but nothing more. And to make any far-reaching forecasts is simply stupid. Therefore, wait while making plans and being jealous of a man for his ex-wife. Perhaps, starting to live with him, you will find something that you yourself will run away from without saying goodbye. Alas, this happens much more often. Your friend may suddenly not like the way your child behaves or something else, and you will be faced with the question of what to do next. After all, telephone communication and rare meetings for several hours are one thing, and living in one apartment is completely different. Therefore, I highly recommend that you think in advance what you will do if the relationship does not work out, and not rush into the pool with your head. After all, you have a small child, and his well-being should, it seems to me, come first.

The availability and fascination of Internet communication has made it a favorite pastime of modern people, for whom this communication can replace real life. It's amazing how many women complain that their husbands prefer virtual sex instead of real sex. On the one hand, it's strange, but on the other... After all, there are new intriguing acquaintances on the Internet, a constant change of impressions, and you don't need to strain at all. Can you compete with your internet girlfriends? Try! If this thought disgusts you, you can console yourself with the fact that the betrayal was virtual and there was no real contact, in the end, just looking at pretty women is not a crime. It turns out that there seems to be nothing to blame her husband for: after all, all this was not really, but "pretend" ... But still, it's worth sounding the alarm if your relationship is deteriorating, and you prefer a computer. And, by the way, virtual girlfriends are also not new in the 21st century, I recall the stormy epistolary novels of poets and writers past ... While their wives were pulling the strap of household chores, the husbands managed to compose not only poems and stories, but also long messages to some sublime lady who shared their subtle poetic impulses.

Sensitive to the complexities of virtual novels, M. Tsvetaeva wrote on March 9, 1923 to B. Pasternak during their famous long exchange of letters with creative confessions and sensual frankness: "If we had met, you would not have recognized me, it would immediately be relieved. In the word I win back, as someday I will win back in that righteous and generous world from the curvature and poverty of this. - Do you understand? "In life, I am immensely wild, I slip out of my hands." And again: "Dear, tear off the heart filled with me. Don't worry. Live. Don't be embarrassed by your wife and son. I give you a complete absolution from everyone and everything. Take everything you can - while you still want to take! Remember that blood is older than us, especially yours, Semite. Don't tame her. Take it all from a lyrical - no, from an epic height! Write or don't write to me about everything as you like. I, besides everything - no, before and after everything (before the first dawn!

And B. Pasternak's answer: "Calm down, my immensely beloved, I love you completely madly, I fell ill yesterday, having written that letter, but I repeat it today. I can't tell you why and why. But that's how it should be. If that for which I sacrifice your voice, your letters and all of myself (except will), consisting in one adoration of you - if this is not a particularity, but the power of fate and height, then this is the business of life and its business to be found among us and let it triumph and its uniqueness, next to ours. Even if this is a particularity, then before the particularity I have a debt, a bottomless debt.

What to say? How did the wife feel, to whom the poet writes such a letter? B. Pasternak to his wife: "I don't feel your feelings with jealousy. I am completely alone now. Marina asked me to stop writing to her, after it turned out that I was writing to her about you and about my feelings for you. It will piss you off too. It's really wild. As if I wrote to her that I love you more than anything in the world. I don't know how it happened. But you don't give any importance to it. Neither bad nor good. We are put side by side with her before we ourselves know where we stand. We are both loved with the same love, before the homogeneity of the air becomes known to us. This is neither taken away nor redone. We tell each other you and we will talk. In your absence, I couldn't help but talk in such a way that she asked me to stop. I did not betray you and did not create a reason to be jealous. In general, did I create anything on purpose, for something or in retaliation to you? I cannot isolate you from the forces that make up my destiny.

I don't have two lives and two destinies. I cannot sacrifice these forces, I cannot defuse fate for you. I would like you to be such a force, one of them. In this case, there would be no confusion, your uniqueness would triumph, and everything would fall into place. But it is also inhuman to think - to allow you, not armed with a great thought or a great feeling, not in the form of a force that composes my fate, into this circle, onto this field. Completely apart from me, you are doomed to constant suffering. I do not want an unequal struggle for you, a brave man with a broad will. You don't deserve to be defeated." I can't defuse fate for you. I would like you to be such a force, one of them. In this case, there would be no confusion, your uniqueness would triumph, and everything would fall into place. But it is also inhuman to think - to allow you, not armed with a great thought or a great feeling, not in the form of a force that composes my fate, into this circle, onto this field. Completely apart from me, you are doomed to constant suffering.

I do not want an unequal struggle for you, a brave man with a broad will. You don't deserve to be defeated." I can't defuse fate for you. I would like you to be such a force, one of them. In this case, there would be no confusion, your uniqueness would triumph, and everything would fall into place. But it is also inhuman to think - to allow you, not armed with a great thought or a great feeling, not in the form of a force that composes my fate, into this circle, onto this field. Completely apart from me, you are doomed to constant suffering. I do not want an unequal struggle for you, a brave man with a broad will. You don't deserve to be defeated." to this field. Completely apart from me, you are doomed to constant suffering. I do not want an unequal struggle for you, a brave man with a broad will. You don't deserve to be defeated." to this field. Completely apart from me, you are doomed to constant suffering. I do not want an unequal struggle for you, a brave man with a broad will. You don't deserve to be defeated."

Is it a betrayal of a spiritual inclination towards another without physical meetings? Perhaps it has to be decided according to the circumstances. A loving husband shares his life with his wife, which means that a virtual romance is able to discuss with her without hiding, otherwise this is no longer the closeness of lovers, but the coexistence of guests of the same yard, cohabitants, what do you think? However, rarely do men in chat rooms look for an opportunity to philosophize and pour out their souls in poetic lines. Most often, this is flirting, frivolous chatter, as well as blood-burning dialogue that turns into "porn" mode. Who took off what at that moment, who would kiss whom where ... What should a non-virtual wife do? Take a mouse in your hands and start a love affair with your husband from another room?

I misplayed it

She recently married her beloved (he is 25), but the honeymoon was overshadowed by a showdown. The fact is that I decided to play my husband: I registered in one social network in the form of a young and spectacular foreigner and began to actively flirt with my then fiancé. I knew how to present myself in such a way that he would be 100% “led”. The correspondence went on for several months. My fiancé and this foreigner agreed that, despite his imminent marriage, they would be able to see each other for spiritual communication and sex (among other things, the husband wrote frank stories to the foreigner about their possible intimate date, and she reciprocated). When, after the wedding, I confessed to my husband that his counterpart was me, he was very angry. He said that I don’t trust him, that I “got into my soul” without asking, that I took advantage of the fact that I know him so well, for your own entertainment and so on. Do you think it is possible to regain his trust? I didn't mean anything bad, it was just a prank...

Alexandra, St. Petersburg, 24 years old

Alyona:

Are you serious? Do you think that you need to ask for forgiveness from your husband and seek his trust now? Do you trust your husband after everything that happened? Do you understand that for a husband, that "foreigner" had nothing to do with you? That he arranged sex with another woman and not with you? Do you understand that what happened is tantamount to finding your fiancé in bed with another girl whom you yourself persuaded to try to seduce him? Even if you provoked this affair, only one thing was of fundamental importance that your fiancé in general, in principle, thinks about the admissibility of connections on the side, given that he marries you. You started a dangerous game, not a prank, and fate gave you a chance to find out the true face of your future husband, and you were so eager to put on a white dress, put on a veil and get the coveted stamp in your passport, that she didn't want to understand what was going on? Do you still not understand that your husband is on fire and is now trying to turn everything upside down? Best defense is attack. But do not be completely naive, and do not believe that only a woman like you, knowing all his weaknesses, could interest him under the guise of a stranger.

A man in love who is serious about marriage and family, his obligations, simply will not get into social networks to communicate with unfamiliar girls. And even more so, he will not develop erotic communication with strangers before the wedding with his girlfriend. But, obviously, 24 years is too little to understand that the fact that this stranger was you yourself does not justify him in any way. That your husband is on fire and is now trying to turn everything upside down? Best defense is attack. But do not be completely naive, and do not believe that only a woman like you, knowing all his weaknesses, could interest him under the guise of a stranger. A man in love who is serious about marriage and family, his obligations, simply will not get into social networks to communicate with unfamiliar girls. And even more so, he will not develop erotic communication with strangers before the wedding with his girlfriend.

But, obviously, 24 years is too little to understand that the fact that this stranger was you yourself does not justify him in any way. That your husband is on fire and is now trying to turn everything upside down? Best defense is attack. But do not be completely naive, and do not believe that only a woman like you, knowing all his weaknesses, could interest him under the guise of a stranger. A man in love who is serious about marriage and family, his obligations, simply will not get into social networks to communicate with unfamiliar girls. And even more so, he will not develop erotic communication with strangers before the wedding with his girlfriend.

But, obviously, 24 years is too little to understand that the fact that this stranger was you yourself does not justify him in any way. A man in love who is serious about marriage and family, his obligations, simply will not get into social networks to communicate with unfamiliar girls. And even more so, he will not develop erotic communication with strangers before the wedding with his girlfriend. But, obviously, 24 years is too little to understand that the fact that this stranger was you yourself does not justify him in any way. A man in love who is serious about marriage and family, his obligations, simply will not get into social networks to communicate with unfamiliar girls. And even more so, he will not develop erotic communication with strangers before the wedding with his girlfriend. But, obviously, 24 years is too little to understand that the fact that this stranger was you yourself does not justify him in any way.

Sergey:

It's interesting how you do it. You, in fact, brought your fiancé to clean water. I found out that he was quite ready to have a mistress and go to the left at the first opportunity. That is, I received one hundred percent confirmation that there will be problems in the future, because the guy does not love you enough to consider you his one and only. After all, he gets acquainted on the Internet with women of broad views and easy behavior now, when romance should seethe with might and main, and he simply should not notice other ladies. But still she married this man and now you even ask how to regain his trust. Did it ever occur to you that he now needs to repent and sprinkle ashes on his head? Why should he apologize and ask for a second chance? To be honest, I feel sorry for you. So far, apparently due to youth, love and inexperience, you don't understand what happened. But, take my word for it, there are a lot of people like your fictional character on the Web. And they are very real. And the fact that you write that you allegedly knew 100% how to seduce a guy is nothing more than your own attempt to justify your husband with at least something. Don't be under any illusions. You're lying to yourself.

I think in your heart you understand very well that a person who is ready to date another woman before marriage woman for the sake of sex and spiritual communication, will find an option for herself in the future. And how are you going to live next to someone who is already looking for spiritual and physical intimacy on the side, I don't know. Why are you needed in this case? Sounds like something is missing from you. What do you think will happen when he finds something in another woman? And if by this time you will already be pregnant or with a small child in your arms? I don't think you got married for nothing. Personally, I wouldn't bet that the marriage would last. So I don't think it's appropriate to return the trust of someone who has already deceived you. After all, you are only untying his hands. Now he is free to do anything, and you can't even say a word about it. In general, I sympathize. And I strongly advise against trying to tie a husband to a child. He does not love or respect you, and therefore, as soon as you get pregnant and purely domestic problems begin, the guy will just run away. And blame everything on you.

Should I take the initiative in sex myself?

I am a beautiful young woman, already the mother of a four-year-old son. After giving birth, I gained weight, but not much. My husband is genetically very thin and is 42 years old. When we began to live together, I was the same as now, everything suited him. Now (apparently, I have a problem) I began to notice that my husband comes to visit the "girls" in the video chat at night, I think you understand what he is doing at that moment. After a serious conversation, he promised me that this would not happen again, everything is fine, but this is so, pampering. And everything would be clear to me if it weren't for sex: everything is okay with him, only he thinks that I should take care of this. I have to take the initiative myself, pull him away from the computer, etc. If not, then I fall asleep without waiting for him, but he doesn't want to wake me up - he feels sorry, as he says. There was silence after that conversation. And now everything is back in the same circle. And I also lost weight after giving birth, minus 16 kg, which my husband did not even notice, he said, it's normal and so, now +5 kg (sorry for the details). What to do?

Ekaterina, Russia, 25 years old

Alyona:

Katya, the problem is that you are only 25, and he is already 42. Unlike you, he has rich experience in dealing with women, and he is convinced that the initiative in sex with a regular partner should come from her, because it will mean that a woman wants and is ready for sex. But if he takes the initiative, then it may look like coercion to have sex, especially if he insists too violently, and the woman at that moment does not want any intimacy. In addition, no one canceled critical days, and wives and cohabitants do not have a calendar hanging on the wall in the bathroom when you can pester her, and when there is a tampon in that important place to be honest, I don't see your issue as a problem. Of course, every young wife is outraged by the fact that her husband can masturbate other people's naked boobs on video, while the missus is bored in the next room. But, Katya, what's stopping you from going to your husband at such a moment and turning your attention to yourself? Women's pride? It should be shown in other situations, not here. The principle works here: if you want a husband, take him warm. And do it with the regularity with which you want sex. There is nothing shameful in this.

This is much nicer and more fun than falling asleep alone in a bed, unsatisfied and offended. And by the way, your claim “why didn’t you wake me up if you wanted sex” is below all criticism. To wake up a wife who is fast asleep just because the man has a "stand up"? This is just from the area of disrespect and coercion: “So what if you were sleeping, but it itches me, and I need...” Imagine. What kind of letters would you write then: “My husband puts his sexual needs above my needs for sleep and rest, if he is impatient, he can wake me up at night and make him satisfy ...” That’s where the horror would be, Katya ... And you, let’s say, there is simply not enough female wisdom and experience to arrange your relationship husband a sexual life for the benefit of both of you. I repeat: there is no problem and will not be if you really initiate sex yourself when you want it, and not wait for your husband to force you to it. And your weight has nothing to do with it ... As well as beauty too.

Sergey:

Catherine, the problem is not with you. I am sure that you look great and, God forbid, you will remain so for a long time. However, with age and years together, the relationship between people inevitably changes. Unfortunately, passion cannot be eternal. And given the fact that men are polygamous by nature, we have to admit that any representative of the strong half of humanity will, after some time, "look" at other women. Especially if sex in the family has become a part of everyday life. That is habitual, standard, practically without emotions. That pulls the men to try something else. What to do with it? Well, for starters, you should just talk frankly with your husband, ask what doesn't suit him in your bed relationship, since he visits a porn chat. Let him say what he lacks. You just need to do this without "arrivals" and accusations. After all, it is quite possible that "everything is OK" for you has become a routine for your spouse. Alas, this happens very often. If again he doesn't explain anything plainly, say that in this case you consider yourself entitled to also look for entertainment on the side. Sometimes, in order to change the attitude to the situation, a person needs to be shown that he can lose something. You can also try to diversify your sexual relationship. Role-playing games, romantic or unusual places for sex and so on. You can contact a sexologist and try to correct the situation with his help. But for starters, it's still worth just talking frankly.

The problem is not even that the husband or wife has virtual romances on the side. The reason they chose to diversify their lives so much is what needs to be understood. Why and why did he or she have such a need? What was missing in family life? Actually, it's not far from treason if virtual acquaintances lead to offline meetings. Not everyone is limited to chatting. And suspicious letters, SMS, calls are a typical set of warning signs that a partner plans to change or has long been leading a parallel sex life.

Cheating is not far off if virtual dating leads to offline meetings. Suspicious letters, SMS, calls are a typical set of warning signs that a partner is planning to change or has been leading a parallel sex life for a long time.

How many wives have become self-taught hackers in pursuit of proof of their husband's infidelity! Truly, detective agencies can rest when a jealous woman steps in. The husband, caught in ICQ, swears that he will "tie up", but it is best to find out from him why he needs all this and what prevents him from doing all this with his own wife. Boost self-esteem by proving to yourself that a lot of girls are happy to chat with him? Get the coveted phone number and meet on neutral territory? Or maybe arouse your jealousy and give the relationship a shake-up for the sake of their revival?

Dating by ICQ

The husband on ICQ gets acquainted with the girls. I, stupid, stuck my nose in and stumbled upon some of them. They talk about different topics ... I told him, and he laughed and said that he was just interested in chatting with them. Do I just have complexes or should I sound the alarm before it's too late?

Happy

Alyona:

We all have complexes. Don't even worry about it. But the desire of your faithful to chat on ICQ with unfamiliar girls instead of spending time with you is worthy of excitement. Well, of course, he laughed at your question. What else was left for him? Honestly admit that you are a read book for him, in fact, and vice versa, and those virtual machines are something new, invigorating his male pride? I hope you asked him what it is interesting for such a married person to chat with strangers. Invite him to chat with you about these topics. No, really. Come and say directly: "Darling, I also want to discuss with you what you talk about with others, don't you think I'm not smart enough for this?" Oh, capture his face for us at this moment, okay? And put the photo in the gallery. But seriously, you know if your husband has lost interest in you so much that he sat down to communicate in ICQ with others, you should think about it. And first of all, at your own expense. Why did he suddenly begin to lack female communication? Why doesn't he prefer, for example, to go with you to a club, to a restaurant, to the cinema or just to the park, to get some fresh air? Maybe you yourself are not very interested in what pleases and excites him, so he is looking for interest in other women? Take my word for it and don't try to check: such dating games are the first step towards breaking off relations due to the banal loss of mutual interest between husband and wife. Today he is "just interested" in communicating with girls virtually, and tomorrow one of them will be interesting for him in real life. Draw conclusions and start changing your routine relationships until his virtual acquaintances turn into real ones.

Such games of dating are the first step towards breaking off relations due to the banal loss of mutual interest between husband and wife.

Sergey:

If the husband began to look for girls for "interesting" communication on the Internet, then nothing good will shine for you. ICQ is not a street, girls don't walk by themselves, and in order to get to know them, you need to make some effort. It's one thing - a general chat, or a forum where everything is in plain sight. And ICQ is a private thing. Almost intimate. Here only radical methods can be used. Moreover, the option with the removal of a large iron box with wires, a keyboard and a monitor in the trash will not work. Then you will definitely get divorced ... As they say, there is a better remedy. Start talking to yourself ... Write down your husband's ICQ on a piece of paper, slip to your friend and knock on him incognito. Get to know each other, chat about what he is interested in, find out what he wants, and ... In short, have you heard or seen Strauss' "The Bat"? Here is... A classic practical guide for a woman in these situations. In general... I can reassure you a little. I know several men among my colleagues who, with the excitement of sexual sex giants, got acquainted with girls via SMS.

We talked, wrote all sorts of smut to each other, agreed on intimate meetings. Yes, but none of them went to these romantic meetings. Maybe your man is the same "giant" with violent disembodied fantasies? So you just at the moments when he powders the brains of girls in ICQ, come up behind ... And then - for children under 18 ... I still don't know a man (impotent do not count) who would exchange good sex with a woman he loves for virtual chatter with anonymous crocodiles . Yes, but none of them went to these romantic meetings. Maybe your man is the same "giant" with violent disembodied fantasies? So you just at the moments when he powders the brains of girls in ICQ, come up behind ... And then - for children under 18 ... I still don't know a man (impotent do not count) who would exchange good sex with a woman he loves for virtual chatter with anonymous crocodiles . Yes, but none of them went to these romantic meetings. Maybe your man is the same "giant" with violent disembodied fantasies? So you just at the moments when he powders the brains of girls in ICQ, come up behind ... And then - for children under 18 ... I still don't know a man (impotent do not count) who would exchange good sex with a woman he loves for virtual chatter with anonymous crocodiles .

Is it worth worrying about a failed betrayal?

I have been married for 16 years and have two children. I recently found out that my husband began to write SMS to his employee ... I know her, I even asked her to provide some services. "Imagine, a check came, and there were no comments on it,"- and before that, as soon as she arrived, the reviews as an employee and a woman were unflattering. She is divorced, has a child, even my age. And my husband always said that he did not understand novels at work. I called her to find out what was the matter. She denied that she already had a man and that she would like to younger. My husband and I are 7 years apart. The husband said that "She did not want to be with me",

"There was nothing, only SMS." Then, at my request, the phone he left at home received the message "Kiss", etc. To which mine said that he could not understand why it had come. I called, clenching my teeth, for the second time and was not shy in expressions, asked me not to interfere in the family, respect myself, take the noodles off my ears, etc. I listened carefully, I hung up the phone first. Mine said that he did not think that I would be so unpleasant because of the failed romance. In many ways he is a good husband, and most importantly, I love him. He asked for forgiveness and not to be kicked out of the house. Now the question is: how to start trusting? I said that I had forgiven, and indeed, my husband began to prove by his behavior that he wanted to be with me, and sex began like on a honeymoon. But all the time a bad thought sits: "What if?" Maybe I'm really, as my husband says, I'm dramatizing everything. And, most importantly, began to talk about acquaintances: who, where, when. "And I'm your faithful husband." He's 43, is this a midlife crisis?

Ksenia, Ukraine, 36 years old

Alyona:

I immediately want to ask: is the husband himself a fool or is he trying to make you look like a fool? Does he himself believe that he is a "faithful husband"? Does he really believe that if he was tritely "not given", despite his courtship, then there is nothing to worry about? If so, then he's a total jerk, sorry. The betrayal did not happen, not because the husband turned out to be morally stable, but because he was given a whip! And the fact that he tells you about the adventures of his acquaintances does not honor either his entourage or himself. I'm sure he envies them. Jealous of how a primitive omega male salivates at the sight of alpha males mating with compliant females. And yours is out of luck. He is denied. That's the whole secret of it "fidelity". The easiest and most reliable way to be faithful to your wife is to be narrow-minded "Omega", which no one even in a nightmare will be seduced by. So, I think you can calm down: no one but you needs such happiness. And, you're right, to some extent it's a midlife crisis. He tried to prove to himself that he had not lost his attraction to other women. But it didn't. Now he's focused on you. Well, it only makes you feel better, I guess. At least your sex life has improved. As for trust, I would not rush here. Moreover, I am sure that now you will have to constantly monitor it. I repeat, he tells you about his acquaintances for a reason. Secretly, he would like to be the same or even better. So the most interesting thing is yet to come. Also because, by the way, that your husband is clearly not one of those who want a change of family.

Sergey:

Middle age crisis? Don't know. May be so. But, rather, the crisis is ripe in your relationship. And therefore, in my opinion, everything that happened only benefited. Both of you took a fresh look at life together and realized that you want to be together. Very well. At least the sex life has clearly improved. In addition, the fear of losing your husband will most likely make you evaluate yourself and those around you more critically, pay attention to your own appearance and, I hope, get prettier. Again, a plus. On the husband, this situation is also likely to have its therapeutic effect. I suppose he realized that his wife is active and in which case you can easily find yourself on the street with a suitcase, but he doesn't want this at all. Therefore, it will become more attentive and legible in communications, so as not to heat up the situation idle. All in all, so far everything is going really well. The muddy swamp of family life was shaken up, and both of you became a little different, looked at each other from a new perspective, began to talk to each other on new topics. Wonderful. I hope everything stays that way and you live happily ever after.

Visitors of "Cleo. RU"who have experienced the features of this kind of sex adventures.

And I once met my husband through ICQ :) We just chatted at first in the evenings, about two months, then curiosity won. And then he had a girlfriend, everything is serious ... So I say from my own experience - this is a dangerous business :)

She

Like everything in this life, he will soon get bored with virtual communication. He will either start dating in real life, or choose another way to distract from reality. In my opinion, nothing terrible happened, the main thing is that you do not let this side of life outweigh the family side.

Kikimora, Bashkortostan, Russia

And because of this asi, I divorced my husband: (I think it was just a clue. I just don't understand one thing: how can you blame a person in a virtual conversation? The text was innocent and childish. And to the one with whom and in what form he communicates, I treated calmly.

Anita

No, ICQ communication is just the tip of the iceberg, but for a lot of people it is the beginning of the end. A person is tired of what is in real life, and he is trying to find someone more interesting. People often "fall in love" in ICQ, and this alone is already enough to destroy a marriage, etc. And then, if a person is looking for communication "on the side", then what prevents him from looking for him not only virtually? I think nothing, and there are a whole bunch of examples. It's a pity.

Natalia

Communication in the virtual is so clear. There we can be "white and fluffy" or "sultry and slender", in general, whoever wants it: either the most real, or the way we dream.

And with loved ones, you still often have to look for compromises and "observe curtseys".

So it's not at all a fact that a person has fallen out of love with you or you are not interested in him, he just wants to relax.

Pauline

I myself also love to communicate very much and I can get to know someone via ICQ, in general, according to my mood ... But if I found out that my husband also gets acquainted via ICQ and talks about nothing, I would be very worried, regarded it's almost like the beginning of a betrayal, because I don't stick with people like that "You can't keep it on a short leash for long." Because over time, this leash will be very much weakened and nothing will be fixed...

***Kulelya,* Moscow, Russia**

And I think that there is nothing wrong with a husband communicating with other women. You can't keep him on a short leash for a long time anyway, and I myself like to communicate :) Only one thing is just communication, and treason is quite another.

Christie

And I have an ICQ affair ... Very serious, I can't live without it anymore, it's my drug. You don't have to pretend to be someone with him, I'm so natural with him, and he never condemns ... He always listens, reassures. But... I am married, he is married and lives in another country... All this is bitter and sad, and as soon as I have the opportunity, I will go to him...

Giselle

Well, progress in the future promises us the invention of virtual reality, which will enter every home and provide us with new opportunities for intrigues. And there will be more and more disputes about what is considered treason, when even touching at a distance will become possible thanks to special devices. Perhaps those who consider the lack of attention and love that were before to be a betrayal are right, and everything else is just a side effect.

Chapter 9

What would happen to us if we took everything and always seriously? So it's time to yearn and believe that life consists exclusively of important matters, one of which is sex. For reproduction, of course. By the way, oddly enough, an overly serious approach to this matter just hurts. Otherwise, why so many stories about women who tried to have a baby for a long time, did everything “according to science”, underwent treatment and calculated a date favorable for conception, and then - in despair - stopped thinking about their desire to get pregnant, relaxed and ... unexpectedly recognized themselves that will soon become a mother? Moreover, sometimes the moment for conception from the point of view of medicine was not very suitable, the conditions are far from perfect, but come on Scientists, as always, have contributed to the study of this issue. Quite a serious study is devoted to how laughter relaxes muscles, promotes the release of the hormone of joy into the blood - endorphin. Isn't sex a source of pleasure and joy? So you can’t spoil sex with laughter, and the public, which cares about everything, just doesn’t condemn such a pastime.

There are always a lot of jokes around sex. In the old days, there were many comic ditties dedicated to one of the main areas of human life. Ethnographic observations have been preserved proving that obscene and indecent ditties in a cheerful form passed on information about the technical side of sex to the next generations. And really, not to open a bicycle to each generation anew? In this way, mistakes will be repeated invariably, and there will be more reasons for quarrels ... No, folk wisdom was also contained in such seemingly frivolous creativity, and how many sayings and signs on this topic were invented! All the modern humor of show programs will fit into one chapter of a collection dedicated to everything that has come down to us from gray times. By the way, at the wedding, late in the evening, under a glass of vodka, especially a lot of such ditties were sung - as an educational program for newlyweds, so the lack of modern means of transmitting information did not interfere with the enlightenment of the young at the moment that was relevant for them. It is interesting that even now teenagers are not too happy to have serious heart-to-heart talks with their parents on immodest topics, where they are very interested in the ironic presentation of information. All the same protective mechanism of the psyche - the frightening unknown is easier to digest in a laughable form.

Joke joke, of course, strife. We perceive the same information in very different ways, each time interpreting other people's actions and words in our own way. However, the boundaries of what is permitted in the intimate sphere, a man and a woman find out everything by the same method.

Trial and error. A fine line passes just somewhere on

the topic of “failures” of a man: this moment causes a lot of negative emotions in men who are always afraid to lose this “main sign of masculinity”, and even in front of witnesses. An attempt to smooth out the tension and calm the husband with a joke is fraught with the danger of going too far. The joke that every hunter sometimes misses, or that "someone's lazy friend decided not to climb today" will not be very appropriate. But how should one react? And the woman wants to show that nothing super-extreme and tragic happened. You have to act very carefully so that it does not work out, like the author of the next letter.

My husband started to "fail"

My husband and I have been together for 10 years. At first, the sex life was very turbulent. Now it's all down to sex on the weekends. I won't say that this is normal, but it seemed to suit both. The husband went on vacation, there was more time, strength and desire. But, surprisingly, he failed. Everyone was joking. Next time again. After some time, she tried to take the initiative herself, he correctly refused. I was confused and had a lot of questions. 1. Is he sick? Then how can I get him to see a doctor? 2. Does he have another woman? 3. Leave everything as it is, do not aggravate, will everything normalize over time?

Lina, 38 years old

Alyona:

The most important thing is not to focus on it. And to reduce the "failure" of her husband as a joke, perhaps, was not worth it. He, of course, laughed along with you, but somewhere inside, "fixed": "I couldn't, became the object of ridicule." Another time, the husband was already subconsciously frightened of his next "failure" and, as a result, failed again. According to sexologists, for a man there is nothing worse than jokes about failure in bed. This programs him to repeat failures. In addition, if the husband has always been "on top" (you write about a stormy sexual family life at the beginning), then it is even more difficult for him to endure failures. Well, if you made the next attempt with thoughts "Come on, let's try to see if it works today," then 99% predicted failure.

And it's not at all necessary that "he is sick" or "he has another". If a man's sexual function is all right, then the presence of another woman is not the cause of sexual weakness in his wife's bed, except perhaps because of remorse (which is rare). In our time, the main culprit of "failures" are stresses, and quite often - on professional grounds.

Maybe it makes sense to talk to your husband, find out how things are at work, is everything in order, is he happy with everything, are you tired ... The inability to be strong, earn enough to cover the needs of the family, low social status (compared to for example, with your old friends, classmates, etc.) - all this can also reduce male potency. In general, there are really a lot of reasons. The main thing is not to rush to "treat" your husband. This can only make the situation worse. Ideally, you would go somewhere on vacation together, change the situation. And if it doesn't work out, then at least on weekends, devote time not to cleaning the apartment and going out to the dacha, but to each other. How long have you and your husband been in some cozy restaurant? And in the cinema? How long have you taken a shower together? How long have you just lay huddled together and dreamed of the future recalled the brightest romantic moments of the past? And by the way, nobody canceled erotic massages to each other.

Sergey:

Well, basically, all three options are possible. True, I would not immediately sprinkle ashes on my head. 10 years is experience. By the way, at the present time considerable. And one of the possible answers - habit - an unpleasant factor, but inevitable. Just do not try to immediately change something in sex. Arranging a striptease or portraying a cat on the hunt is an honor, but if this has not happened before, then most likely it will cause a strange and by no means positive reaction. Although ... Laughter prolongs life. But I think it's time for you to change. Not just to be repainted in a radically black Titanic, but to change internally. If you haven't played sports, do it. Find something for yourself what will be interesting and important. And at the same time, involve your husband in these activities. I started talking about sports only because when you see the results of training, you become more confident, more fun and liberated. In addition, self-esteem is greatly increased from classes. Maybe someone will not agree with me, but, in my opinion, a man should feel that he has achieved something, done something. Therefore, when sex becomes a routine, and not only sex, then all interest is lost. Be unreachable. Trite "don't give" for a while. When doing the same fitness, you can easily refer to fatigue after a workout. Let the husband himself feel the desire. And he will begin to achieve. After all, you are a woman. It should want you. Just do not invent anything superfluous, such as other women. Even if so, you can change the situation, only by looking at it with different eyes, that is, by changing. That's probably how it is. Good luck.

Romance is romance, but excessive seriousness in bed prevents you from relaxing and just having fun. Funny situations in sex happen from time to time for everyone, and only a sense of humor helps to avoid embarrassment. People who do not know each other well, or who are not very familiar with sex due to inexperience, or who simply treat each episode of their life as something extremely important, attaching too much importance to trifles, can perceive the ridiculous accidents that accompany intimacy, almost tragically. The fear of being ridiculous in someone's eyes makes you avoid any embarrassment, fetters a person in those moments when you can and should relax and stop playing social roles.

In theory, close friends, relatives, and even more so spouses should trust each other and accept each other for who they are. If we do not choose relatives, and therefore it is not always possible to get along with them, then friends and a husband are those who are close to us in spirit and interests. Have you noticed how it can be almost impossible to establish contact with some people, there is nothing to talk about with them, or their reactions to your words and actions are unpleasant? But these people also have their own social circle and those who love them. People are very different, and therefore it is all the more valuable that you can come to a close friend and calmly tell her about your feelings and thoughts, without fear of ridicule and condemnation, hoping for understanding and advice. Ideally, the spouses are just as frank with each other and even more, especially since they have the most common interests - the well-being of the family. And trust grows just from the confidence that in any situation, the husband and wife will support each other.

In bed, that trust is just as important. How can you relax and get maximum pleasure if in bed we will "keep face" in front of our husband, all the time afraid of his condemnation for the wrong movement or word? True, everyone has a taboo in the intimate sphere of life, something that causes a negative reaction. But even this reaction should be restrained, translated into a joke, otherwise no one will dare to offer something new, and predictable sex will become insipid over many years. Therefore, every innovation, in general, everything that frightens, can and should be dressed in a comic form. if in bed we "keep face" in front of our husband, all the time we are afraid of his condemnation for the wrong movement or word? True, everyone has a taboo in the intimate sphere of life, something that causes a negative reaction. But even this reaction should be restrained, translated into a joke, otherwise no one will dare to offer something new, and predictable sex will become insipid over many years. Therefore, every innovation, in general, everything that frightens, can and should be dressed in a comic form. if in bed we "keep face" in front of our husband, all the time we are afraid of his condemnation for the wrong movement or word? True, everyone has a taboo in the intimate sphere of life, something that causes a negative reaction. But even this reaction should be restrained, translated into a joke, otherwise no one will dare to offer something new, and predictable sex will become insipid over many years. Therefore, every innovation, in general, everything that frightens, can and should be dressed in a comic form.

Each innovation, in general, everything that frightens, can and should be dressed in a comic form.

He annoys me with his behavior

Not a single day passes calmly ... My boyfriend and I have been living together for six months. Since we moved, our relationship has changed 180 degrees. We fight every day. I began to notice that he annoys me with his behavior, movements, tomfoolery and many others. He can sit and eat and annoy me, he can sing a song and I can get mad. And when he becomes serious and says serious things, I'm just drawn to him, I can kiss, hug and not let go. But he is practically not serious you will see, he is like a child ... Maybe this means that I do not love him?

Alyn, Canada, 23

Alyona:

This may mean that, on the one hand, you are holding on to this guy because "every 23-year-old girl should already have a boyfriend", and here, of course, logic works

"It is better to have a tit in your hands"... But, on the other hand, you yourself understand that this option is not exactly what you need. And so, in order to resolve this contradiction, you are trying to bring the existing version of a potential husband into line with your ideas about what you need. But, alas, at the same time you forget that in front of you is a living person, and not a blank from which you can cut a wooden man to your taste. Do you think that you have the right to spoil a guy's mood, to show undisguised hostility towards him, to behave towards him as a mentor just because you deigned to choose him as a potential life partner? Who gave you such a right? Imagine you would live with a person who would not be satisfied with you the way you are? And whenever you would like to be yourself, he would insult you, pulled, and forced to behave differently? Would you be happy? Would you think that this person loves you? Or would you doubt that they love you, and not some of their interests, which are strangely connected with your presence in the life of this person? In general, in my opinion, it is better to be around an intelligent person who knows how to talk about serious things, but at the same time has a good sense of humor, is relaxed, open and cheerful, can afford to fool around and is not afraid to look funny, than to live with a smart bore .

In my opinion, this suggests that your relationship and you yourself are developing, growing up. Unfortunately, not always the first relationship grows into something more than just the first relationship. And often this happens because girls mature earlier than boys. This trend is especially visible in recent years. And when some become already young women who need a family, the seriousness and responsibility of a partner, the latter are still boys who do not want to treat life in any proper way. As a result, couples break up, because instead of a man and a woman, a mother and a son appear in them. So your boyfriend, most likely, already evokes in you more maternal feelings than partner ones. After all, notice that you yourself write that at first the guy infuriates you when he behaves like a child, and as soon as he becomes more serious, you hug him, kiss. Remember, you are his, not he you. That is, you are already teaching him, as a mother teaches children. For bad behavior - punishment, for good - stroking, encouragement. And since this situation already ceases to suit you, most likely, in the near future you will scatter. What will happen next, I do not know. If the guy has enough brains to become more serious, then perhaps the relationship will resume. If not, then someone more suitable will appear in your life. And there is nothing terrible in this. That's life. Relationship will resume. If not, then someone more suitable will appear in your life. And there is nothing terrible in this. That's life. Relationship will resume. If not, then someone more suitable will appear in your life. And there is nothing terrible in this. That's life.

Let's see what the difference between ridicule and joke is. Ridicule humiliates one of those present. The joke does not humiliate, it only makes you look at the situation from the side, through the eyes of an outsider, in order to understand that everything that is happening is not so serious as to be too upset. Laughter as a defense mechanism has long been known to people. Hence the popularity of comedies, clowning and any form of entertainment that causes fun. In medieval culture, carnivals became especially popular - when, wearing a mask, anyone could have fun for several days, removing themselves from social roles, trying on others, entering into an atmosphere of jokes and fun. And in the days of the Inquisition and helpless medicine, this was an outlet for all segments of the population, a way to compensate for tension and stiffness in normal times, when much was under prohibition and life was full of dangers.

Now we unconsciously continue to use irony, jokes, smiles as a way to improve relationships, relieve tension in an unfamiliar environment, a way to unite a company of unfamiliar people.

In bed, jokes and laughter are a way to smooth over minor setbacks, bring the other half into a cheerful mood and help to relax. Anyone who takes sex too seriously and believes that it is a sacrament and a sacrament that must be strictly regulated, which must be taken seriously and "try" all the time so that everything works out perfectly, will be surprised by this approach. How so? Are laughter and romance compatible? In films, passion is also portrayed with music that is quite tense, almost tragic, to show that real sex and passion is something great and should not be reduced by inappropriate laughter. But in reality, every time for many years this is impossible and even ... boring.

I am the wife of a football fan.

My husband and I dated for five years and were married for five years. The child is two years old. I'm on maternity leave. The husband works a lot (there are business trips), if possible, helps with the child. My problem is that my husband, after a week-long business trip (not an easy job), crossing the threshold of the house, hugging me and kissing the child, runs to the TV and turns on the sports channel or Sports box on the computer. If he is reminded of himself, then he returns to the family, if not, he can watch football until late at night. Gathering with friends in cafes, he will definitely ask to turn on football, and he is no longer with us. I feel deprived of his attention, as if football is the main thing in his life. Of course, he says that he loves, all sorts of compliments, sometimes very passionate, but after Chelsea beat someone there. It may, of course, seem that this is not a problem at all, but this hobby of his has squeezed something very important out of our lives - evenings spent together, heart-to-heart conversations, he now has no time for this. Promising a child to take a walk, he can abruptly postpone everything because of a very important match (which does not fit in my head and repels me very much). I tried to join this sport in order to somehow get closer and begin to understand my husband. I can't pretend that I'm interested. I tried to distract him with fishnet stockings ... He did his job during the break between matches (according to Shurik).

I don't know how to react further. I really hate this kind of neglect. Of particular interest is the man's opinion on this matter. Can abruptly postpone everything because of a very important match (which does not fit in my head and repels me very much). I tried to join this sport in order to somehow get closer and begin to understand my husband. I can't pretend that I'm interested. I tried to distract him with fishnet stockings ... He did his job during the break between matches (according to Shurik). I don't know how to react further. I really hate this kind of neglect. Of particular interest is the man's opinion on this matter. Can abruptly postpone everything because of a very important match (which does not fit in my head and repels me very much). I tried to join this sport in order to somehow get closer and begin to understand my husband. I can't pretend that I'm interested. I tried to distract him with fishnet stockings ... He did his job during the break between matches (according to Shurik). I don't know how to react further. I really hate this kind of neglect. Of particular interest is the man's opinion on this matter.

Olga, Voronezh, 30 years old

Alyona:

It is necessary not to react, but to sit opposite each other and discuss the current situation. On the one hand, every person has the right to be passionate about something, and your husband is no exception. He really likes football, and this should be taken for granted, especially considering the fact that he probably did not become a football fan in the last couple of years and you got married with your eyes open. On the other hand, you need to explain to your husband that at some point he goes too far, shifting values and not even thinking about the fact that a child is more important than any football match. Your husband is absolutely wrong to think that communication with the child can be postponed until later, and the match cannot be missed. Just the opposite. The match can be watched in the recording, and many times. But the time lost in communication with your child can never be returned to anyone. Children grow up fast, faster than we would like, and soon the time will come when the child will no longer need to communicate with his parents, and after a while the children and parents will change places. And, in my opinion, it is necessary to focus on this: whatever it may be, but a man in a family is first of all a husband and father, and only then a football fan. And nothing else. It is necessary convey to your husband: he did not just get carried away with his hobby, he postponed his family "for later" because of him.

If your husband is, in principle, a reasonable, but addicted person, offer him to draw up a schedule: on which days there is a broadcast of matches that he cannot miss, and on which days he will be completely tolerated. Agree with him that you go to a cafe or a bar only when there are no very interesting football matches in order to spend time with each other, and not with the TV. Agree that if he promises to take the child for a walk, then this means that there can be no other cases, no force majeure, and no sudden football matches (which is basically impossible, since this is always planned in advance).In general, in my opinion, you, two adults, need to sit down and seriously discuss everything, without swearing, without blaming. Apparently, love still lives in your family, it's just that your husband got carried away and forgot.

Sergey:

I believe that every person should have the right to something personal. Someone is fond of fishing, someone is football, and someone is macramé. No, of course, I understand that you would like your husband to be completely absorbed in you. But trust me, it will only get worse. And besides, it will no longer be your husband. After all, you have been living together for quite a long time, and your husband has always been just that. Now you unilaterally suddenly decided to change the rules of the game. I'm afraid he won't agree. Therefore, I would suggest to moderate the requirements somewhat. The man loves football, well, nice. Indeed, in this, in addition to some disadvantages, there are many advantages. At least you always know where to find him in case of emergency, and these places have nothing to do with other women. At the same time, I agree that it is bad manners to refuse a promised child. But this is easier to deal with. For example, such moments can be severely suppressed. That is, to put an ultimatum: dad said dad did, otherwise divorce and maiden name. I think once will be enough for a man to start looking at the schedule of games before making promises. Other than that, you can't really change it. Either accept the situation as it is, or leave.

Only with experience comes an understanding of how you can joke and what will hurt your partner. Everyone has different boundaries and ideas about what is permitted. These boundaries have to be constantly studied in family life in the first months, and then either expanded, or bypassed, or not gone beyond them. But within the framework of what seems acceptable to both of you, there is a certain freedom of action. What restrictions can be placed on jokes and pranks? What will hurt your partner and what won't? Only the study of his character, the experience of communicating with him will tell. Well, in the end, it didn't work out to make you laugh - sorry, and that's the end of it. Life is so complicated and long that such trifles should not spoil your mood. But successful jokes will not only defuse the situation, but will become a pleasant memory. Believe me, you can forget the super successful sex, but the funny incidents associated with it

It is not necessary to tell someone else about what happened to you, but together you can remember what happened many years later.

Sex jokes are often associated with getting a new experience. Therefore, in youth there are especially many of them, due to inexperience, people manage to say or do something ridiculous, but this - with the benevolent support of a partner or partner - becomes just a funny case in life. Otherwise, there is tension in relationships, and even complexes for the whole next life.

Especially a lot of funny things happen in sex according to the principle “parents behind the wall” (sex in the park, car, forest, etc.) - forced or spontaneous, reckless, when stress, fear of being discovered are mixed with excitement and pleasure from the process. Feelings are sharper, and if in the end they noticed you, but did not catch up - yes, remember this funny. Or, in a hurry, you spread your jacket on an anthill and found it already at the peak of passion - yes ... What does not happen in a life rich in adventure! And for a long time you still feel like conspirators and wink at each other at other people's stories about similar cases.

Spontaneous funny incidents are one thing, but "home-made" is something else, but no less intriguing. The husband puts on your clothes, you - his, and what happens from this role-playing game is up to you. How exciting it is to imagine yourself as someone else and try new behaviors with your loved one, knowing that this game is just as interesting for him! All these ideas of "getting to know each other again", playing nurse or teacher, cause a lot of laughter and give you a chance to look at each other in a new way.

... Both reached such heights of love skill that when their passionate ardor was exhausted, they extracted everything they could from fatigue. Indulging in the pagan adoration of their bodies, they discovered that love, in moments of satiety, has many more untapped possibilities than desire. While Aurelian rubbed egg white into Amaranth Ursula's tight nipples or rubbed coconut oil on her firm thighs and fluffy belly, she had fun with his mighty child, played with him like a doll, painted round clown eyes with lipstick, and eyebrow pencil - mustache, like a Turk, tied ties of satin ribbons, tried on hats made of silver paper.

Gabriel Garcia Marquez. One hundred years of solitude

We joke, but do not offend. In general, it is not difficult. Imagine yourself in the place of your husband and think about whether he will like your joke, whether it will cause offense. Although ... Sometimes you can't guess the reaction. Only if you adhere to a strict sequence of actions all the time and repeat the same thing in bed all the time, you will get tired of yourself and cause discouragement for both. But after the comedy that you watched in an embrace, there is surprisingly relaxed and pleasant sex.

What jokes are inappropriate in bed? Making fun of the partner's shortcomings; anecdotes in the process (somehow distracting, does not allow you to focus on sensations);

– Political jokes (out of place, set in a serious mood).

Are his intentions serious?

My boyfriend and I have been dating for about two months. A week after they started dating, he (he's 27) said he loves me (I'm 23), and since then he hasn't stopped mentioning children in conversations (laughs about this, asks how many children I want, a girl or a boy and etc.). He says he wants to live with me. Talks about the future, including me (uses "we"). In addition, he constantly talks about marriage (jokingly). And yesterday he put on a performance! He said that he was divorced and that he had a son, and whether I agreed that his son called me mom, etc., and whether my attitude towards him would change because of this. And then he asked if I was ready to marry him (I said yes). After a 10-minute conversation, he suddenly laughed: he invented everything ... He has a rich imagination! By the way, he jokes all the time about everything. He is very well endowed and his family too (I didn't meet with my family, since they live in South Korea, he is Korean, he has been working here for several years). His mother is here on vacation, and he does not introduce me to her, and my parents do not know about me. Wants his father to inherit his company. Apparently, he is afraid that our relationship can somehow affect the decision of his father, since my boyfriend is also a journalist, and he does not want his personal life to come out. But according to conversations, he wants me to move to Korea with him. Is he serious about me? What does all this "around the bush" mean? That our relationship can somehow affect the decision of the father, since my boyfriend is also a journalist, and he does not want his personal life to come out. But according to conversations, he wants me to move to Korea with him. Is he serious about me? What does all this "around the bush" mean? That our relationship can somehow affect the decision of the father, since my boyfriend is also a journalist, and he does not want his personal life to come out. But according to conversations, he wants me to move to Korea with him. Is he serious about me? What does all this "around the bush" mean?

Daria, Israel, 23 years old

Alyona:

I don't think the guy has any intentions for you at all. Well, except for one thing - how to mock the simple-minded fool that you diligently portray, believing everything he tells you. I think it amuses him a lot. Do you really believe that your two-month-old boyfriend is the heir to your dad's Korean millions? Do you really think that a young man who is going to inherit the family business will master the profession of an international journalist, instead of studying economics, marketing and the like? Do you really believe that a dad who plans to transfer the business to his son will allow his son at 27 to do such nonsense (from the point of view of a business person) as writing in newspapers? What should the son of a South Korean oligarch do in Israel for several years, and even as a journalist? Do you think, that it's natural to propose to a girl two months after they met, but at the same time hide her from her family so that, God forbid, mom and dad of a 27-year-old boy don't know about you? And who in general can be interested in the personal life of a South Korean journalist in Israel? Is he a rising star on CNN or the BBC? But even so, who cares about his woman?

I'm afraid you don't know anything about your boyfriend at all, and he's just exercising his fantasy with you. I am sure that I will not be mistaken in the fact that he does not hold you for a smart girl. And he has no serious intentions and cannot be. There is this type of guy: they start relationships with girls to put them to bed, and for this they come up with a lot of impressive "facts" of their biography, and since they don't take these relationships seriously from the beginning, the lies turn out to be arrogant, shameless and from this very believable for the victims. So I would advise you to be careful with your new boyfriend. He's either just playing or a pathological liar. At the very least, check him out. Although I won't be surprised if you don't even know his real name yet ... So I would not be in a hurry to pack my bags to South Korea. Your boyfriend is a dark horse.

Sergey:

In my opinion, it is not necessary yet to draw any serious conclusions. Indeed, besides the fact that the guy is rather frivolous about your relationship, he is also a representative of a completely different culture. For two months of communication it is impossible to understand what it means to live in a different cultural model. In addition, you are just dating and are not connected by a common life. So I don't know why you suddenly agree to marriage proposals so quickly, but I would not advise you to rush. You don't know this person at all. No matter how suddenly it turned out that the man is actually married, has a bunch of kids, and on the Promised Land he just relaxes with a young, ingenuous girl. Therefore, do not build castles in the air. A young man who is serious about you will do serious things. In the meantime, between you only "hee hee" and jokes, no need to build far-reaching plans.

By the way, why don't you joke back? Say that you talked to your parents, that they agree to give their blessing on your marriage, but only after the man is circumcised. This must be done tomorrow, dad agreed on everything. And look at his reaction. Just be as serious as possible. You can also say that you told dad about your relationship and that you were proposed, and dad asks for the phone of the groom's parents to start negotiations about the wedding. And if he doesn't, tell him that dad will find everything himself, because he is very serious. And when your boyfriend runs to the door, forgetting to get dressed, say that you were joking. What if he can and you can't? But I think that after that the man himself will roll off. Until the jokes are over. Why don't you joke back? Say that you talked to your parents, that they agree to give their blessing on your marriage, but only after the man is circumcised. This must be done tomorrow, dad agreed on everything. And look at his reaction. Just be as serious as possible.

You can also say that you told dad about your relationship and that you were proposed, and dad asks for the phone of the groom's parents to start negotiations about the wedding. And if he doesn’t, tell him that dad will find everything himself, because he is very serious. And when your boyfriend runs to the door, forgetting to get dressed, say that you were joking. What if he can and you can't? But I think that after that the man himself will roll off. Until the jokes are over. Why don't you joke back? Say that you talked to your parents, that they agree to give their blessing on your marriage, but only after the man is circumcised. This must be done tomorrow, dad agreed on everything. And look at his reaction. Just be as serious as possible. You can also say that you told dad about your relationship and that you were proposed, and dad asks for the phone of the groom's parents to start negotiations about the wedding. And if he doesn’t, tell him that dad will find everything himself, because he is very serious. And when your boyfriend runs to the door, forgetting to get dressed, say that you were joking. What if he can and you can't? But I think that after that the man himself will roll off. Until the jokes are over.

But only after the man is circumcised. This must be done tomorrow, dad agreed on everything. And look at his reaction. Just be as serious as possible. You can also say that you told dad about your relationship and that you were proposed, and dad asks for the phone of the groom's parents to start negotiations about the wedding. And if he doesn't, tell him that dad will find everything himself, because he is very serious. And when your boyfriend runs to the door, forgetting to get dressed, say that you were joking. What if he can and you can't? But I think that after that the man himself will roll off. Until the jokes are over. But only after the man is circumcised. This must be done tomorrow, dad agreed on everything. And look at his reaction. Just be as serious as possible. You can also say that you told dad about your relationship and that you were proposed, and dad asks for the phone of the groom's parents to start negotiations about the wedding. And if he doesn't, tell him that dad will find everything himself, because he is very serious. And when your boyfriend runs to the door, forgetting to get dressed, say that you were joking. What if he can and you can't? But I think that after that the man himself will roll off.

Until the jokes are over. That they made you an offer, and dad asks you to give the phone of the groom's parents in order to start negotiations about the wedding. And if he doesn't, tell him that dad will find everything himself, because he is very serious. And when your boyfriend runs to the door, forgetting to get dressed, say that you were joking. What if he can and you can't? But I think that after that the man himself will roll off. Until the jokes are over. That they made you an offer, and dad asks you to give the phone of the groom's parents in order to start negotiations about the wedding. And if he doesn't, tell him that dad will find everything himself, because he is very serious. And when your boyfriend runs to the door, forgetting to get dressed, say that you were joking. What if he can and you can't? But I think that after that the man himself will roll off. Until the jokes are over.

The secret of lovers who know a lot about caresses: when laughing, the vagina involuntarily contracts, which causes very interesting sensations in a man in the process (and the woman too). True, coughing works the same way, but laughter is much more pleasant, don't you agree? So include in your arsenal of tickling and funny nicknames, smeared with whipped cream to your heart's content! By the way, let's think about sex toys again. Not only does their very appearance at first evoke episodes from comedies and makes you laugh, but there are also especially funny things in the form of Mickey Mouse, Homer Simpson, or some other cartoon character.

By the way, couples in love do not forget to joke about sex outside of bed. The kitchen is another source of entertainment and a few more years of life thanks to healthy laughter. Chasing around the dinner table after your wife with a banana and serving phallic still life's for dinner, putting on one apron from all your clothes and experimenting with the composition of dishes, you can have fun and smoothly reduce kitchen twists and turns to love games. And all these intimate jokes, notes, a special language of half-hints that is born when children appear - all this brings together and sets in a playful way.

And psychologists also note that sincere laughter is an indicator of the openness of character, which means that such a person is more liberated in sex. And in principle, a happy person laughs more often. So, even in happy moments alone with your husband, do not be afraid of the desire to laugh, because this is the laughter of joy and satisfaction with life. Merry nights to you and mutual love!

Conclusion

Sex Instructions for use

Sex (or its absence) has a great influence on everyone, they talk and write about it, joke and argue ... At the state level, they seriously solve the problems of propaganda, abuse and other things directly related to sex, but how much is connected with it indirectly! From childbearing to ulterior motives for changing careers, and if you believe the old Freud, it turns out that the driving force behind creativity is actually the desire to relieve excess sexual tension in a different form.

It is useless to scold or hate universal human instincts, to strive to deny their presence in our lives or to make them the cause of failures - in general, too. The main thing is to use what nature has given us with pleasure, without striving for self-flagellation because of the ways in which you get this very pleasure.

Due to numerous stereotypes, sex is often turned into a problem, the cause of tragedies or a farce, but is it worth making your whole life so addicted to sex that you spend months and years worrying about some kind of failure in sex, its lack or disharmony in intimate relationships? ? Do not worry, but look for the best solution. Identify the cause of anxiety, talk with your beloved man (woman), study the theory, and visit a doctor if necessary.

It is very useful to understand exactly how sexual instincts affect the behavior of the people around you, why exactly you do not feel satisfied or are constantly on edge, and what brings you real pleasure. Managing your desires will help you avoid unpleasant stories when it turns out that the man next to you is unworthy, when you find yourself in bed with a man, and then painfully regret what happened. Agree, such situations happen sometimes with frightening constancy. To avoid disappointment, you need to be able to feel your intuition and correctly understand the reactions of your body. It will tell you how much it is worth approaching a new acquaintance, it will make it clear whether your closeness with him will be pleasant. Even at the stage of kisses and first touches, this is felt, if you do not rush and adequately evaluate everything, without being distracted by social status and other external factors. Sleep something you not with status?

Oddly enough at first glance, sex is something that also needs to be learned. What for?

To know this manifestation of life, to comprehend your own body and soul, so as not to get bored during the thousandth sexual intercourse with your spouse and not to look for new sensations on the side, upsetting your loved one when these new sensations are available to you, if you show imagination. However, sex is a mutual matter, pleasure depends not only on you alone. And, by the way, one of the manifestations of mutual love, and therefore depends on the emotional component of your relationship. Love is the desire to please each other, and sex is one of the pleasures, so marriage without good, enjoyable sex for both is nonsense. Answering for the thousandth time the question of whether it is possible to enjoy sex with a husband in a long-term marriage, one thing can be said: if after 10–20 years you are still bored together, there is something to talk about and why live together,

Well, ideas will be thrown to you by life, the Internet, books, including ours. Keep an eye out for the Cleo website, where the Two Opinions section receives thousands of letters every week from readers who share their concerns and ask for advice.

www.ingramcontent.com/pod-product-compliance
Lightning Source LLC
LaVergne TN
LVHW012042160826
845678LV00014B/2678